ENGLISH HERITAGE

CASTLES

TOM McNEILL

BATSFORD

ACKNOWLEDGMENTS

First published in the United Kingdom in 2006
by Batsford
151 Freston Road
London
W10 6TH

An imprint of Anova Books Company Ltd

Copyright © Batsford
Text copyright © Tom McNeill

The moral right of the author has been asserted.

ISBN-13 9780713489934
ISBN-10 0 7134 8993 6

A CIP catalogue record for this book is available
from the British Library.

10 9 8 7 6 5 4 3 2 1

Reproduction by Classicscan
Printed in Singapore by Kyodo Printing Co. Ltd

This book can be ordered direct from the
publisher at the website: www.anovabooks.com,
or try your local bookshop

Distributed in the United States and Canada by
Sterling Publishing Co., 387 Park Avenue South,
New York, NY 10016, USA

To my two families, the one which brought
me up, and the one which looks after me now.

I would like to thank a number of individuals and institutions who have supplied
illustrations: Figures **2** (1000209041), **9** (1010611011), **57** (1000102031), **60**
(1008252021) and **93** (1006801051) permission British Library. Figures **8**, **13**,
16, **21**, **22**, **40a**, **53**, **70**, **75**, **86**, **88**, **89**, **94** Cadw. Crown Copyright. Figure **46**
reproduced courtesy *The Archaeological Journal.* Figures **17**, **18**, **19**, **23**, **29**, **32**,
36, **38**, **39**, **40**, **45**, **49**, **51**, **54**, **58**, **66**, **67**, **71**, **73**, **74**, **78**, **81**, **83**, **84**, **87**, **91**,
95, **96**, **97**, **98**, **100**, **101**, **102** and **103** were supplied by the author. All other
photographs, including the reconstruction drawings, come from the collections
held by English Heritage, with particular thanks to Chris Evans for figures **27**, **30**,
35, **59**, **76**, **77** and **85**; Maura Pringle for figures **1** and **72**; Barrie Hartwell for
figure **56** and **101**; and Gill Alexander for figure **92**.

CONTENTS

PREFACE

There has been a plethora of books on castles over the years, not least over the last two decades; why, therefore, reissue one? The main reason must lie in the nature of castles themselves. There are many views of them because they were such complex structures. Had they been built for a single purpose, or even for one purpose at a time, it would be easy to summarize our knowledge of them in a book. As it is, it is inevitable that different people will find different aspects of castles that they want to stress, rather than the ones that are already in print. For example, some authors have written a chronological story to stress the line, or lines, of the development of castles; what the standards of fashion and design were at any given time. The topic of excavation has been well covered by J R Kenyon in his book on the subject, while timber castles are the subject of a book by P Barker and R A Higham. The place of castles in the general settlement of the land, in relationship to towns and villages has been studied by O Creighton and R Liddiard, opening up a whole new area of thought. P Dixon and P Marshal have provided a series of studies on the ceremony and formality of the internal arrangements of castles. Different authors have struck a different balance in their accounts between the castle during war and the castle during peace: C Coulson and M Johnson have stressed the formality of castle defences as opposed to their effectiveness. A Wheatley has considered their literary role. Each viewpoint provides a rather different account, even of the same castle, let alone of castles as a whole.

This book was written from a different angle, to try and explain castles for the modern visitor to them. So far from being a rival to these or others, I hope that this book will cover questions which are less emphasized elsewhere. I have chosen not to follow a chronological line in this book, because I have never liked the task of putting buildings, which seem to me to be so interesting mainly because they are so individual, into a sequence of development. The variability of castles impresses us with the range of choices that a prospective castle builder was faced with. This seems to me one way to appreciate castles for the complicated buildings that they were, to acknowledge the choices, whether of site, expense, display or military defence, which went into their design. If the Middle Ages were anything, they were a time in our past when the men who controlled so much of the land, also controlled so much of government and society directly. Nothing symbolizes this lordship better than the castles that they built, not only to live in, but also to control their estates, and the country. How they planned their castles tells us much of how they organized their life, and therefore the lives of the many people who depended on them.

It seemed a reasonable aim to combine this view of the castle as a busy work place, literally a powerhouse, with an explanation of how a castle might be understood by a visitor to its modern remains. Castle designs were not haphazard, but were the result of a series of decisions about how the building would serve the purpose for which it was planned. Much of the evidence for the use of castles, both in the days of their use and now, must inevitably lie above ground, in the arrangement of their rooms and features. This has led me to concentrate on two types of castle in this book. The first is those castles built in stone, rather than those of timber, simply because of preservation. The second is those castles with standing remains preserved above the original ground level, as opposed to those that we know mainly from excavated foundations and remains.

No one comes to have knowledge or views on anything alone. I find it an invidious and hopeless task to pick out those who have helped me in whatever I have learned about the subject. In point of time, I am glad to acknowledge the primacy of my debt to Professor Martyn Jope and to Peter Addyman, who first introduced me to serious castle studies. I have been privileged to attend the meetings of the Castle Studies Group in the British Isles, and those of the Château Gaillard Colloquia on the Continent. At these meetings, I have been able to learn so much from all the participants that I could not list them here; I trust they will forgive me if I have been so convinced of their arguments that I now think of them as mine, although I may contribute errors all of my own. Finally, I must acknowledge many years of students. There is no discipline like that of having to explain one's views to them for clarifying the problem bits, and many a student has taken a suggestion from me and made it into the serious line of research it had not been previously.

1   LORDS AND MEN

One of the things that make castles interesting is that they are all different. Primarily this is because they were built by men of differing ranks, at different times, in different regions of the British Isles. In the corn lands of the south and east of Britain, the kings of England and Scotland stood at the head of society. Below them were ranged grades of the landed aristocracy, from their own families through the general ranks of the earls and barons to the knights and local or county gentry. These ranks changed with time. In the earlier part of our period, the grades were blurred and indistinct, with a relatively large baronage merging into the knightly class, and intermarrying with the royal families. By the end, in the 16th century, the baronage, or nobility, was more closely circumscribed and defined, cutting it off from the knights below; younger sons did not automatically count as lords. The origins of the aristocracies of England and of Europe were complex. One root was in the Germanic warrior chiefs who succeeded to the Roman Empire. Later came the warlords who emerged after the attacks of Vikings and others in the 9th and 10th centuries. In England, of course, the latest layer resulted from the Norman Conquest of 1066. In this process, the kings do not appear as particularly different from the greater aristocrats, just as the differences of titles that emerged in the 11th or 12th centuries, earl, count, duke or lord were not reflections of accurate assessments of their actual wealth or standing. In many ways, kings were originally simply super barons.

In the north and west, something of the older order, dating from before the 10th century, survived. Many of the lords retained the titles and the status of the petty kings of the post-Roman era. There was not the same system of power extending down from kings to grades of landed aristocrats and so down to the peasantry marshalled in villages dominated by lords and dedicated to the large-scale growing of corn. In time both 'systems' changed. In the north and west, Welsh, Scottish and Irish lords imitated the European, English model of lordship, with its elaborate and stable dependent hierarchies and the increasing power of kings. 12th-century Scottish kings brought in aristocrats from England (often younger sons with few prospects at home) who knew the new ways of management and could help them transform their own power as they did their own. A little later, after 1169, English aristocrats also

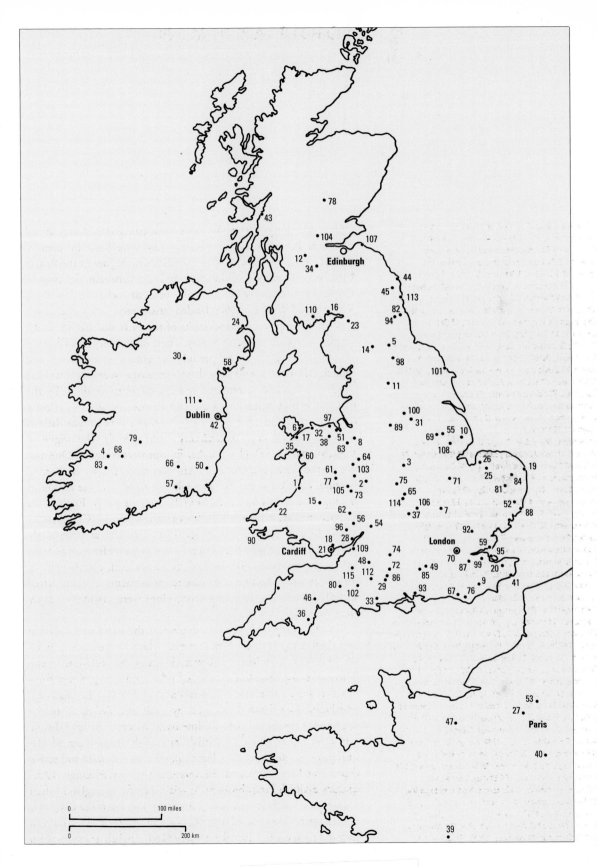

Edinburgh

78

43

104   107

12
34

110   16

24   23

44
45
113
82
94

14   5
98

101

11

30

58

100

111
42   97   31
89

Dublin

6   55   10
17   32   69
79   38   51   8   108
4   68   63
35   64
83   60   26
66   50   61   103   25   19
77   2   3   84
1   105   73   75   81
15   65   114   52
62   106   37   7   88
22   56
96   54   92
90   28   59
18   109   74   London   95
Cardiff   21   70   20
48   72   87   99
115   112   86   49
80   102   29   85   93   67   76   9   41
33   39

46
36

53
27

47   Paris

40

39

0   100 miles

0   200 km

came over to Ireland and, by a mixture of invitation, conquest and inheritance, set themselves up as a second aristocracy to the native lineages. Later medieval European aristocracies became very self-conscious about their membership. In this England and Scotland differed from the rest of north-western Europe, where all the sons of a noble were counted noble, so that the class tended to proliferate and at the same time merge into the gentry.

Whatever the roots of the aristocracy, they all obeyed a common code, central to which was to display their wealth. They did this traditionally, in the old non-Roman societies principally through hospitality, entertaining their followers and allies with feasts, and through the clothes and ornaments they wore. These traditional lords owed their power to the ancestry (genealogy was crucial to their support) and to such practices as hostage-taking, while later lordship was based more on landed resources. The nature of display also shifted, from portable wealth to permanent centres. The people of the Middle Ages set great store by building – as we can see in their legacy of great churches and other buildings – and they expected the centres of lords to reflect their wealth and power, which is the root of castle building. This is the origin of castles; they were built to provide lords with an appropriate place from which to exercise control over their lordship and to display the power it gave them. Their lordship varied, their circumstances varied through time, their resources varied and so the castles they built varied in size, in fashion and in elaboration.

LORDSHIP

These men had one thing in common: they were all lords. Their lordship varied as much as the sorts or degrees of men that they were. Historians have labelled the organizing of power through a hierarchy of the holding of land in return for service, as seen in the kingdoms of England and Scotland, as the feudal system. Power here depended on the granting of land in the first place, with rights of control and the enforcement of law going along with the grant of the land. In theory, the king owned all the land, but delegated areas down to others, who in turn granted out parcels to their subordinates, and so on down to the actual workers of the land. The holders of land expected that their sons and heirs would inherit their land when they died, and indeed a holder of land could rely on doing so for ever as long as he performed the duties demanded of him when he was first granted the land. Overwhelmingly in the upper classes, the core of these duties related to military matters. In all cases, the lords both retained some land to be worked directly as farms for their own profit, the so-called demesne land, and released some to tenants. Especially after the population decline of the 14th century, many lords gave up direct farming in favour of money rents. They still were concerned to maintain their pre-eminent position in the politics of the country, through the domination of the area that they considered should be under their control. In the north-west, the lordships were not feudal in their origin, nor in the basis of their power. Instead of land, the ultimate means of power was through the control of people, often organized through kinship groups. A lord's muster roll rather than his rent roll was what counted.

Lordship in the Middle Ages was personal. The exercise of power through the paid bureaucracies of the Roman Empire or modern states was essentially alien to the medieval world. A man acted through his immediate social inferiors, who were bound to him through ties of relationships that went back over generations. To be effective, a lord must carry with him the good will, or at least the acceptance, of his principal subordinates. This is most clearly described in the realm of national politics: for example, King Edward III of England was successful where his father and grandson failed largely because he and his barons worked closely together. The modern argument that co-operation is ultimately more efficient than confrontation in management would have been seen as an expression of good lordship. This lordship required personal contact between the parties. A medieval lord, be he a feudal baron of 11th-century England, or a Scottish Highland chief, needed to meet his men regularly and to discuss affairs directly with them. Absentee lords, such as English barons who inherited lands in Ireland or the Welsh marches, soon found that their power in those lands slipped away from them.

In all cases, political lordship was the essential business of the medieval aristocracy. To be a medieval lord, therefore, meant leading an active life of lordship. In a hereditary society, some lords will obviously be much more effective and efficient than others, but none could opt out of lordship and see their position survive.

2 *(above)* Sir Geoffrey Luttrell depicted in his psalter, in the way he wanted to be recognized as a mounted warrior.

Lordship, in the sense of the powers and responsibilities involved, was part of their personal possessions, usually to be inherited and passed on to their heirs in turn. It went with the property, with land or a region that the lord traditionally controlled. To do so, he needed a base in the area concerned, so that he could exercise the power and influence that he considered his right over the men of the district. Violence was always a possibility, and the root of the aristocrats' power was their prowess in war (**2**, **3**). The bases naturally, therefore, reflected their owners' military role, and were more or less fortified. Out of this dual role came the castle; a place where a lord could live and exercise his power through personal contact with the principal men of the area, and a fortification to protect him from attack or as an expression of the threat that underpinned his power.

Lordship had its boundaries. At one end was the power of the feudal kings, who commanded the resources of more than one country in the case of the Plantagenet kings of England, with their possessions in France and elsewhere. They owned more castles than they ever needed to live in, or indeed could hope to visit at all regularly: in 1214 King John had over a hundred castles in the British Isles and France. Many of these were in parts of his lands which he rarely visited, if ever; they were the seats of royal deputies rather than of the king himself. A king needed a far greater number of administrators to manage his kingdom than a baron did to organize his barony; this was not just a question of the size of the two areas of control, but a matter of the kinds of

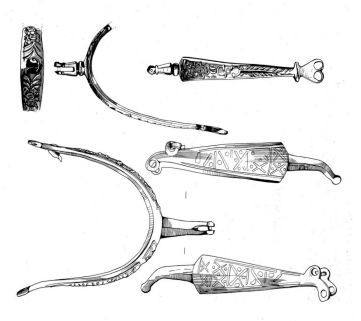

3 *(right)* Spurs from Beeston castle; essential for medieval horsemanship but decorated as symbols of lordly wealth and power.

powers each possessed. At the same time, the development of royal government encouraged some of the departments to take up residence away from the castle where the king might be and lead a separate existence.

At the other end of the feudal scale were the holders of one or a few manors, gentry or knights who simply did not have the resources for building or maintaining a large stone castle. In the late Middle Ages (the 14th and 15th centuries) these men lived in what we now term manor houses, with a hall and buildings enclosed like a castle, but without the array of power proper to a true castle. The tower houses of Scotland and Ireland may be seen as a mirror image of the manor houses of the English countryside. They were built by a similar class of men, but often without providing accommodation for a full administrative household. Between the kings and the builders of manor houses lay the ranks of the feudal baronage, the core of the men responsible for most castles. As well as the differences of rank, lords and lordship varied with time. The most obvious of the developments was in the nature of power. In England after the Norman Conquest of 1066, or in the Wales of the 11th- and 12th-century Norman Marcher lords, the power base of military conquest was overt. So, too, was the direct relationship between the structure of society and the grants of land held by each man; men performed duties in direct proportion to their land, and farmed much of it themselves. The 14th century saw a major change throughout Europe, with a collapse of the population that had been growing steadily, indeed rapidly, since the 10th century.

Farming land for corn was much less profitable, and lords responded by leasing much of it out. The steady advance of royal power from the 12th century onwards had made small-scale fighting between rival lords much rarer. Force and the direct obligations of tenantry were replaced by the manipulation of royal offices and justice, and by subtler pressures on the men of an area. These differences, together with other forces, such as the rising costs of building castles as standards steadily rose, meant changes in the role of the castles themselves. The heart of their role always remained, however, that they were there to accommodate a lord and his household so that he might carry on his lordship over the area under his control.

THE LORD'S FAMILY

Nowadays we think of a man's wife and family as forming the innermost core of his life and, indeed, of making up his essential household. In part this is because most of us do not work at home, but this is only part of one of the differences between the pattern of modern men's lives and those of the lords of castles. A lord did not usually marry until he had at least come of age, and either inherited land or had some share of his father's land settled on him. A girl, on the other hand, was normally married in her teens. Often, therefore, a lord was considerably older than his wife. Given the patterns of their ages, and the dangers either of war or childbirth, it is clear how many lords, and their ladies, survived their partners to marry more than once. Certainly their first marriages, and even later ones, were arranged for them, as part of the business of politics or land inheritance. Parents or guardians were expected to take the compatibility of the two spouses into consideration, but this was always likely to be a secondary issue. A man married for policy not personal affection.

A lord who married a lady did so to gain control of her lands, and vice versa; he had to settle on her a marriage portion, usually of a third of his lands, which she retained for life. His wife was therefore always, at least in theory, in charge of an estate of her own. One of the basic facts of life is that lands need to be administered and so a lady needed an administrative structure to provide income and to keep them intact. Her own personal needs, most obviously the clothes she wore as befitted her status, required servants of her own; again obviously these must have been maids. A lady was therefore the centre of a second group of people in her own right, rather than simply as part of her husband's household. This was not purely a formal arrangement, for formidably independent ladies are scattered throughout the history of the Middle Ages. In times of crisis, or when he was away, they would deputize for their husbands. They came into their own in widowhood: the death of Gilbert, Earl of Gloucester in 1295 (he was 47) left his wife, Joan, a widow of 23. She successfully defied everyone, in particular her father, King Edward I, and married one of her late husband's squires, Ralph de Monthermer in 1297: they lived happily for ten years, with Ralph acting as Earl through the right of his wife, until Joan died in 1307.

One of the problems of describing the society of the Middle Ages is the small amount of evidence for children and childhood. Like wives, they appear in contemporary accounts principally as elements in the dynastic successions of their families. Royal children had separate households in which they grew up, often apart from their parents, in the care initially of nurses and then of tutors or guardians. Aristocratic children had social equals unlike royalty, and this dictated their lives. Between the ages of five and ten, they were sent away to the household of another lord who brought them up and trained them in the skills they would need in later life. They came to visit their parents at intervals, and of course returned in their late teens to take up their places as full members of the next generation of the family.

To judge from the surviving financial accounts, the lives of the royal children were dominated by clothes and horses. There are a few personal details, such as the small cart bought as a toy for Edward I's son Henry in 1274. Likewise toys are remarkably rare in the archaeological record. It is too much to expect unbroken wooden toys to survive (children being as they are) but we would expect to find parts such as the wheels of Henry's little cart. We might expect baked clay figurines (soldiers perhaps) or marbles to survive yet they do not. Horses were not the same as a bicycle for a modern child, a deluxe toy, but rather a necessary part of their training. A large part of their early years must have been spent mastering horsemanship, which was vital in later life. From the 13th century at least, a lord would have had to be literate in the

4 *(above)* Cutaway reconstruction of Acton Burnell castle showing the stores, hall, chambers and chapel at the core of a castle.

modern sense (medieval men seem to have used the word to mean fluent in Latin, or even to have a degree) to administer his estates and to play his part in national or local government as a lord was expected to. The myth of the illiterate baron dies hard, but myth it is, at least from the 13th century. As with the lady of the castle, the presence of children must have been a frequent if not constant part of the life of a castle, but one which called for its own establishment – a nursery or school for the well-born children fostered in the larger household. The sources that we have stress the separation of the lord from his wife and children. Lords were often absent, visiting other possessions or away on state business or at war. This, together with the business base to the marriage, makes it easy to assume that his family (in the modern sense of wife and children) played little part in a lord's life. This is a very limited view. Time and again it is clear that lords placed considerable trust in their wives, either in their advice or to act for them in their absences, which hardly implies any lack of respect or even affection. Similarly, one of the less pleasant customs of medieval kings was to exact hostages from their barons, almost always their children. The pressure involved may not have been affection but honour, and some fathers will always have taken the line, like William Marshal's father is said to have, when King Stephen threatened his hostage son with death, that he could get plenty more where William came from. This said, genuine feeling must have played a part.

THE LORD'S HOUSEHOLD

If the lord's family life was not the core of the castle's existence, the lord himself was. To carry out his work, and keep control of his lands, he needed body servants to look after his personal needs, and men to carry out or enforce his decisions. This provides us with the essence of the lord's household as we see it in the early 12th century, either royal or baronial. The officials are also the servants, for the lord did not distinguish between the two areas. Providing food and drink were the jobs of the seneschal (also called a 'dapifer' or steward) and the butler, under whose control were the controllers of the larder, pantry (for bread: French *pain*) and buttery (for bottles: French *bouteille*) and the kitchen with its cooks; there was also a serving staff. The lord slept in a chamber, where he also wisely kept his valuables, literally in a chest under the bed. The man in charge was the chamberlain, under him in the royal household came the treasurer, and generally a staff of ushers to control the doors, and others to serve and look after the clothes. Also in the 12th-century English royal household, there was a third major official, the chancellor, in charge of the chapel and the whole apparatus of written records, and so the law; significantly this was the first 'department' to leave immediate attendance at the mobile royal court and settle down permanently at Westminster (see **2**).

These men formed the true inner core of the castle population. Quite soon in any household, but above all in the English king's, they became hereditary posts and their holders tended to perform their duties only on major ceremonial occasions or by deputy; even by a deputy for a deputy. This tendency and the inevitable growth in bureaucracy led to a demand for more rooms for the lord's officials (**5**). They were too important to do the actual duties, but they were happy to remember the source of their power: two families of Scottish nobles were the Stewarts and the Durwards, in origin stewards and door guards; the Earls of Ormond in Ireland were butlers. In baronial households the chapel and clerks rarely took on the importance of the royal Chancery: the two key men were the steward and the chamberlain or treasurer. Beyond this inner core of these two and their staff came the next layer, usually to be seen as of lesser status and even pay, the constable and the marshal. They were responsible for the security of the castle and its people, the garrison and the porters, and for the horses and outdoor servants, such as the carters

5 *(below)* Reconstruction of a tower at Bolingbroke castle with individual rooms for members of the lord's household.

and the huntsmen. Both also rose to great political importance in the royal households, because of their essential military roles, but in baronial ones seem to have been of rather lesser status.

No two households were precisely alike nor were the duties described anything like water-tight. Any servant of the lord might be asked to do any task, if he was simply the only man available at the moment; this was after all a regime of personal lordship. That should not hide the fact that, however the household might be arranged in detail, the basic structure of each was similar. From the beginning there were various 'departments', each under an officer with a staff below him. These divisions were based on aspects of the lord's daily life and also the physical layout of his castle; the inner core of hall, chamber, chapel and service, with an outer circle of the courtyard and the world beyond. His family could fit into the inner circle if it was with him, as another of the elements, his wife's circle of ladies and servants, and the children's establishment, in the same sort of position as one of the officers.

It is important to emphasize that the major officers of a lord were not far below him in social status (**6, 7**). From the beginning of castles and the lordship associated with them, we find the lord having a group of his principal supporters with him. It was their duty and privilege to attend him and to help him with their advice whenever he made major decisions. Royal officers were drawn, as we have seen, from the ranks of the higher baronage. Whenever the sources allow us, we find the major lords of the century after the Norman Conquest of England, such as the Clares, consulting an inner group of their tenants, just as the king consulted his barons. In both cases, the more land that the man held, the more likely it was that the lord would seek his support, but there were always a few lesser men also present, presumably because of their personal qualities of experience or intelligence. Medieval lordship could never function for any length of time without the consent and support of the men of the stratum below, whether a king and his magnates, a baron and his knights, or even a manorial lord and his richer peasants. This was not in any sense democratic, but simply recognition of the limits of practical power without a large bureaucracy as well: tyranny is never simple to organize.

The development of households was steady through the Middle Ages, as the power of the aristocracy grew more stable and their life became more complicated. The 12th-century household developed with time, according to the needs of the lords. In England the emphasis was on bureaucratic elaboration and control of finances. The single office of steward was split into two by the later 13th century, with the emergence of the estate structure and the development of the record keeping. Land management and relations between the lord and his tenants became the job of the steward, and finances the preserve of the treasurer. Concern for better financial control dictated that in the 13th-century household there would be a second steward to oversee the purchase of food, drink and other requirements, and then to supervise their use by the various officials. The food itself was the concern of the cook, butler and pantler, responsible to the steward, with a man, often termed a marshal, responsible for the serving staff in hall. The household steward takes his position below the estate steward and the treasurer in the hierarchy of the English baronial household by the end of the 13th century. By contrast, in the more violent areas of Wales or Ireland, the constable or marshal responsible for soldiers appears along with the others, in a structure more like that of 12th-century England.

The king of Scotland occupied a position of wealth approximately similar to that of an English magnate, with the additional powers and responsibilities of kingship. His household is described in a document of about 1300, a central date to our period. The chancellor was primarily a state official, with a clerk of the rolls to keep control of the charters and writs. The chamberlain was responsible both for finance, with a staff of auditors, and for the governing of the household as a whole. This last he did in the first instance through the steward standing at the head of the immediate household, and the constable, who was responsible for guarding the king. The marshal was responsible for discipline and also for the whole organization of the hall, through an under-marshal (the modern butler). An almoner controlled the royal charity: four chief clerks controlled the supplies. As well as these, it is stated that the offices of pantler, butler, larderer, baker, naperer, chandler, waterer, etc, which had been hereditary in the past, were now performed by a deputy. It must be noted that these are simply the major officers; there is no mention of the men who did the actual cooking or serving of food, or those who cleared up or looked after the horses, hounds, etc. of the household, nor of personal servants of any of the major officials.

6 (above) Aerial view of Farleigh Hungerford castle, the home of the Hungerford family, stewards to the Dukes of Lancaster; service in the household brought honour.

7 (below) Aerial view of Edlingham castle, a reward to the Feltons' for fighting in France; the site is now away from any other settlement.

The 14th and 15th centuries saw the confirmation of the position of the household steward, usually known now as the chamberlain, in the baronial household, who came to be the third major official after the estates steward (the steward, *par excellence*) and treasurer. Partly this was a consequence of the general habit of lords to withdraw from the boisterous camaraderie of life in the hall to the relative peace of their chambers for most of their daily life. The purchase of food tended to be organized through a specialist clerk, with the cook and the butler (or marshal) overseeing the preparation and service. The chapel staff, as befits their obvious specialization, forms another group of people.

Outside, the horses were still the responsibility of another major official, the marshal of the earlier periods. From this period we have formal descriptions of the organization of magnate households rather than having to deduce their arrangements from indirect sources. They have two tendencies: to exaggerate the precision of the departmental divisions that they describe, and to ignore the numbers of people who did much of the actual work as opposed to those who organized it and were responsible for expenditure.

At the same time lords became more sedentary in their habits, partly perhaps as a result of the shift away from direct demesne farming to rents; in the 12th and 13th centuries it made more sense to travel around and eat the produce of their farms where they were gathered in. This, and the increasing elaboration of their lifestyles, led to three sections in the magnate households. There was what one might term the core: the essential inner household and officials. Located at the formal chief castle of his lordship was a wide network of supporting staff that supplied the more complicated things from the home estates, such as leather, cloth or beer. To the inner household was added on great occasions what could be called a lord's riding household, which was composed of those men, his

8 *(above)* View of Caerphilly castle from the east, with its extensive water defences securing the lordship of the area.

retainers, whom he could call on for support, whether political, military or for show. All three elements would be present at key points in a lord's life, but not by any means always.

No sooner has a historian described a situation than he must qualify it. Away from the royal centres of power, there were differences. In the lordship of Glamorgan, in the border lands between England and Wales, the Clare lords administered the courts – a lord of the March had almost all the powers of the king in law – raised revenue, and carried out either the defence of his lands against the Welsh or the conquest of more, with the aid of a group of his principal tenants who served as his officials, paid or unpaid (**8**). In Ireland the 13th-century lords, with less legal power but with the advantage of remoteness from Westminster, also acted through their major tenants who held the offices of stewards, treasurers or sheriffs in their lordships. Equally, in England from the 14th century onwards, the lord's council tended to become even more formalized in its composition. It consisted of three groups of men: the estates steward, treasurer and other principal officials; lawyers paid a fee for their advice; and the heads of families tied to the lord often through their ancestors and through the tenancies of land. These were the men who would advise not just on whether a proposed line of action was legal or not, or could be administratively efficient, but on the wider questions of the implications for the lord's relationships throughout his lordship, or how it would affect his standing and honour in the world of his peers. This council was not the same as a lord's household, because it was not more or less permanently attendant on him, but he called it together when he needed to. In royal terms, the same core of advice and support emerges from the Great Councils into the institution of Parliament in the later 13th century. A lord in residence in a castle will have been either accompanied there by such men or else be met there by them. An allied reason for a lord to visit any castle was to meet the principal tenants of the locality. This was partly in the narrow interests of business, but also as part of the social pattern of life which involved a lord meeting his men, hearing their views on all sorts of topics and mixing with them, making them feel involved in the larger world which he represented.

HOW MANY PEOPLE LIVED IN A CASTLE?

If we approach the question of the personnel and structure of the household of a lord from the point of view of its organization, then we will tend to stress the emergence of formal officials such as stewards and treasurers. On the other hand, from the point of view of social class the distinction is less clear. These officials were drawn from the same class of people as had always advised lords, their principal tenants, or the rank just below the lord concerned. The reason is clear. Most of the business involved the management of land and the tenancies of the estate. It makes sense to draw your advisers from the class of men who are brought up to manage lands of their own; if you want to manage men in a class-conscious world it is much better to use men of the same class. They will instinctively know what is acceptable as a rule, and if they come from the group of tenants of the lordship itself, they will know the individuals and family backgrounds as well: they may be too close to them to be efficient reformers but they will know their disputes and problems well and so avoid conflict. This was the hallmark of successful medieval management; consensus and the reinforcement of the status quo rather than detailed schemes for efficiency.

The second means by which the tenants of a lord were drawn to his castle was because one of the duties they owed him for his land was that they should help to guard his castle. Because it was a part of their tenancies, we hear of the richer men, the knights and sergeants. Their numbers and organization varied. In the 12th century a garrison was found for the royal castle of Windsor from 73 knights: each owed 40 days of service, so that nine were on duty at any one time. The baronial castle of Richmond, well away from royal power in the south, had a garrison drawn from 187 knights, each of whom owed two months service: we know the period of most of them, and together with those whose dates are unknown, we can see that there should always have been 31 knights on duty. A 14th-century drawing (**9**) shows the posts of eight of these men, the constable at the gate and the chamberlain near the hall; we do not know the reasons why the other six were chosen. By the end of the 13th century most of these duties had been transformed into payments of money, but the services demanded were real until then. The numbers that we can cite are too small; they represent only the officers, and there must have been other men employed either by the lord directly, or else brought along by the knights. These are figures for times of peace, core garrisons which would be reinforced if time and money permitted, when there was a threat of war and siege.

There is no way we could answer the question: how many people lived in a castle, or how many men did it take to garrison a castle? Apart from the fact that they are all different, it is just as impossible to give the answer for any individual castle, other than for a certain day when a document might give us the basis for a guess. Such a guess would only be for one day, and would be different for the next. Odiham castle was an important centre for Simon de Montfort in 1265 at the height of his civil war with Henry III. His wife, Eleanor, spent most of the year there, with a household of under a hundred people. On 19 March Simon arrived with a train of 161 extra horses, and presumably a similar number of men. The most obvious variation in numbers in a castle was whether the lord was there or not. If he was, he brought his household and attracted all the officials and visitors there; if he was away, the castle went down to a 'care and maintenance' basis, with a constable, a minimal garrison and some servants. The presence of the lord's steward to hold his court would bring more people to the castle, but nothing like the arrival of the lord himself. The more important visitors and officials, men of knightly rank perhaps, would bring their own servants with them when they were at the castle. If the visitor were a baron then of course his sizeable household would accompany him.

The people living in a castle were thus naturally organized into groups or units. The lord and his family, his officials and servants and his visitors all made up atoms that linked together into the molecules of inner or outer households or the total number of people in the castle (**10**). The officials of a medieval lord's household took their titles from buildings or rooms in a castle, such

9 *(right)* A 14th-century drawing of Richmond castle, showing the flags of some of the knights bound to serve as officers of the castle garrison.

as the chamber, buttery, pantry and kitchen. Within this framework it is easy to see how individuals' roles could be varied at short notice, taking on or shedding part of their work at the lord's will: there could be nothing pre-ordained about their functions. The physical arrangement of the castle was equally accretive over much of its history, with individual elements added within the circuit at will. There could be no absolute agreement either on the precise number of rooms required or of their arrangement. Always, however, it is possible to see the physical units that the social groups required: the central rooms for the main public life of the lord, his own lodgings and those of his wife, suites or rooms for officials and the buildings for the supporting cast of servants of every sort.

Castles were empty places without their lord's presence, literally and metaphorically. When he was there they came alive in a confusion of people and noise, as a hundred or more people crowded in. The noise would have been exacerbated by the normal arrangement of buildings all facing onto one or more central yard. It cannot have been helped by the multilingual nature of medieval society. In England, as in the rest of the British Isles and Europe, the upper classes spoke French until the later 14th century. Townsmen and villagers spoke Middle English, while the upper clergy, such as a lord's chaplain or the household of a visiting bishop or abbot, might well have talked naturally in Latin. In parts of Wales, Scotland or Ireland, there would have been a significant element of Celtic speakers as well, peasantry or native nobility.

10 *(above)* Aerial view of Portchester castle from the south. The inner court of the castle occupies the north-west corner of the Roman fort, which formed the outer court containing a small priory among other buildings. It was set beside the sea because the king used it on his way to France.

11 *(below)* The decorated forebuilding of the great tower at Castle Rising. Erected as a celebration of the marriage of William de Albini with the widow of King Henry I, the outer walls of the entry stairs are decorated with the latest motifs.

Two species dominated castle life: men and horses. The number of horses, whether for riding or for carriage, was always large, and their quality varied from the great war horses to good riding horses and down to cart horses. The society was also overwhelmingly masculine. Only the lady of the castle, or a visiting lady, had women attendants or servants, other than such occasional assistants as laundresses. Even married servants and officials seem to have kept their wives elsewhere, outside the castle, unless they had a role in the lady's entourage. Given the crowded nature of the accommodation, it was probably best for everyone, especially the women themselves, if they kept away.

Castles were very complicated places. Each one had to accommodate a different sort of household, according to the standing and ambitions of its lord and this would change through time with the different owners' wishes and abilities. Each site was physically different, and the resources of each lord varied. There could be no such thing as a standard castle, as there could be a standard fort for the Roman army: medieval building style tended to stress the individual variety in castles as well as churches, so that there could be no uniformity of style such as Palladian houses display. Each castle represents a complex balance between the site, the need for defence or the show of it, and accommodation. Both defensive ideas and living standards varied over the years, so that a castle was liable to incessant change to keep it up to date (**11**). Each change presented a new twist to the balance of features. The buildings that resulted can be read as a series of choices or decisions about the sort of life the lord wished to lead, or the sort of appearance he wished display. Castles were not only splendid buildings in their own right but they were the self-conscious frames for the lives of their builders. This frame also extended well beyond the rooms for the lord, to the service buildings to support the complex, to the enclosure and through the parks and gardens to the whole landscape.

2 BUILDING CASTLES

A man who began building a castle was embarking on a large undertaking; what it involved is the subject of this chapter. Obviously the first choice was where to build it. Often, particularly as time wore on, this was a question of rebuilding an existing castle rather than starting a new one on a 'green field' site. But all castles had to start at some point, and so we shall concentrate first on how and why a man might choose a particular site. The origin of castles on continental Europe is a controversial topic, and can only be very briefly summarized. It appears, in northern France at least, to have been a two-stage process. Firstly came the larger castles sited at important existing administrative centres: stone towers with halls for ceremony and entertaining such as at Loches, whose start is now firmly dated to the 1020s, and Doué la Fontaine by the river Loire, or Burg Broich in the Rhineland. Later came a proliferation of lesser castles as the tenants of the major lords seized control of the villages that they held, at times in an attempt to free themselves from the conditions of tenure. We can also see lesser castles being established away from the main centres, along with new settlements, in a colonizing of peripheral areas of forest or other wasteland. In either case, the castles act either to reinforce the existing patterns of settlement or to expand them into new areas. They serve to graft lordship on to an existing structure rather than to create a new one; lordship comes first with castles to reinforce it.

CHOOSING A NEW SITE

The British Isles provides a different scene; here a new aristocracy introduced the castle as part of the forcible seizure of land. In these circumstances it is natural to think that castles, which are after all warlike structures, should have been sited in order to reinforce the conquests, according to a strategic plan, like the forts of the Roman army in Britain after its conquest, or the Hanoverian forts in the Highlands of Scotland in the 18th century. These were built on new sites to control lines of communication, and to provide garrisons of sufficient size to go out and confront large numbers of hostile inhabitants or invaders. The ultimate examples of this nature must be Hadrian's Wall, or the defences of the south coast of England from the Napoleonic wars onwards.

In England after 1066, William the Conqueror's victory over the Old English state established a new Norman regime. The

12 *(right)* Map of castles built in England during the generation after 1066. They are concentrated in the existing county towns, to reinforce the seizure of power.

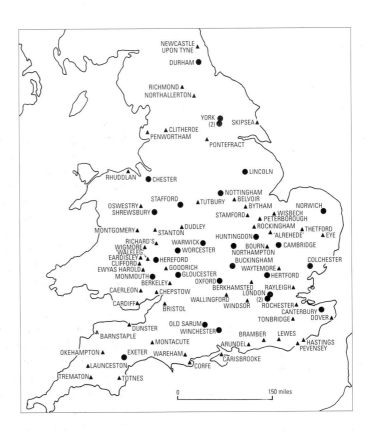

Normans introduced to England as part of their conquest a new kind of fortification, the castle. This statement has been challenged recently, but neither of the sites suggested as built by English lords as opposed to Normans who came to England before 1066, Goltho and Sulgrave, have seriously fortified enclosures, as was recognized by their new owners after 1066 when both were significantly strengthened. Our knowledge of where castles were built in the generation after 1066 in England is biased towards the royal castles, but the choice of site is interesting. William concentrated his building on the county towns, to control the existing centres of power; apart from these castles, there is a surprisingly small number known (**12**).

There are some hints of a purely military type of fortification among the castles built after 1066. The earliest forms of castle were large enclosures built by some of the most important men in William the Conqueror's entourage. These provided the space for a large body of troops, and their long perimeter must have needed a sizeable garrison for their defence. When Robert of Mortain built the castle of Neroche, Alan of Brittany that of Richmond (see **25**), or the Conqueror's half-brother, Odo of Bayeux those of Deddington

13 *(above)* Chepstow castle seen from across the river Wye. The first great tower is still the dominant building; the buildings to the left were added by Roger Bigod in the late 13th century.

and Rochester, all large enclosure castles, they were keeping their household knights together around them. Later these castles were equipped with a strong point, either a motte of earth or a stone keep, which could be defended by a much smaller number of men as the knights were dispersed by being granted lands in the surrounding countryside, leaving the castle to the immediate household of the lord. At Chepstow (**13**) William fitz Osbern had a strong stone hall as the nucleus of his castle from the beginning; at Castle Acre William de Warenne built what was in effect a lightly defended, but large, country house as the first castle on the site. The major barons of William's conquest – and all these men belonged to the first rank of William's court – did not necessarily see it as essential to have a large garrison in their castles, even in the years after 1066.

Some of the sites they chose were militarily strong, either tactically, in that they are well defended by nature all round, or strategically in that they may be said to control points of communication. Chepstow is set on a high cliff over the river Wye, just above its junction with the Severn and it is a key point of entry from England into south Wales, so it fulfils both requirements. Richmond and Neroche are both set at the tops of high hills or cliffs, defended on at least one side from attack. Castle Acre is sited where the Peddar's Way crosses the little river Nar (**14**), but this is no real obstacle. If the crossing is significant to the castle, it is because it makes the castle convenient to reach rather than because the castle might impede hostile forces at the crossing; they would simply walk across it elsewhere. Rochester castle was sited in a poor defensive position in the corner of the Roman town defences (which Odo buried in his new bank), but it was placed close to the crossing point of the Medway river (see **70**), Deddington was sited at the crest of a steep slope, which protected one side, but the others

14 *(above)* Aerial view of Castle Acre. The castle is set beside the crossing of the river Nar, just visible at the top right of the picture, and the regular streets of the new town laid out to serve it.

were easily accessible, and there are many other similar sites in the area. Edward, sheriff of Wiltshire, built a strongly defended enclosure for his castle of Ludgershall, but it is sited on flat ground in no sort of defensive position, when the scarp of the Wiltshire Downs was available within a mile of his chosen site.

The crucial factor in all these sites, except Chepstow, does not appear to have been any abstract military strategy: the main reason for choosing a site was apparently convenience. William de Warenne's choice of Castle Acre is particularly interesting, for it is in contrast to his castle of Lewes. This is set on a hill overlooking the estuary of the river Ouse as it goes through a gap in the Sussex Downs. It was the head place of the 'Rape' of Lewes, one of the districts created by William, apparently to safeguard the routes from England to Normandy. Lewes was sited for military reasons, while Castle Acre was chosen because it was a convenient centre for William's estates in East Anglia. Similarly, Odo may have chosen Rochester as the site of one of his major castles for strategic reasons, but he picked Deddington because it was at the centre of many of his estates. The selection of these sites was not done in a vacuum. They were all places that were already occupied and were, in some sense at least, centres of population. The new lords of England after 1066 did not intend to change the way people lived on their new lordships, farming and paying rent; they were primarily concerned with the ownership of the lands. One factor is clear: very few, if any, were built in the open countryside. William's castles were mostly built in towns and his barons did the same, even if it meant founding a town, as we shall see. In some cases there are indications that the sites were chosen for their symbolism, because they were old places of high prestige; the most obvious of these is the placing of castles in former Roman towns and forts. The reason for this may be more mundane; they had part of the enclosure already built. Similarly, some mottes may be sited on earlier mounds, either for symbolic reasons, or simply because it made obvious sense to modify and re-use an existing mound.

CASTLES IN THE CELTIC LANDS

It was different when the Anglo-Normans or English (call them what you will) expanded outside the kingdom of England into Wales, Scotland and Ireland. In Wales the struggle was always a question of piecemeal military conquest by individual barons at first, setting up lordships one at a time and defending them against internal revolt and external attack by Welsh princes or other lords, until the English king completed the process with the conquest of north Wales. In Scotland during the 12th century the Scottish king made a policy of attracting English barons to the country and granting them lordships and lands to hold under his authority. This was part of a plan to transform his kingdom along the lines of the rest of Europe, and also to expand it into independent areas, such as Galloway or the Highlands. Ireland saw a mixture, from the late 12th century, of invitation by native kings, seizure of lands by individual barons, and attempts at control and expansion by the king of England.

Chepstow was meant to be part of the expansion of William fitz Osbern's lordship into Wales. This was a pattern repeated over the next two hundred years by the English lords in Wales. Castles such as Pembroke, Cardigan and Aberystwyth, in the 12th century, mark the attempts to found new lordships, the first stage of which was to build a castle in a strong military position. By the end of the 12th century the Welsh princes had appreciated that one way to hold on to their ancestral land (or land which they too had conquered) was to build a castle on it. Criccieth castle shows both processes (**16**). It was built by three Princes of Gwynedd and then adapted by Edward I after his conquest. The pattern of castle building in Scotland was different, being much more associated with the reorganization of lordship, influenced by the royal power. Instead of new lordships established through conquest, they were established through the power of the king. In the heart of his kingdom, the south-east of the present country, where the king was strong, few castles were built (see **18**). It was on the fringes that we see the combination of the establishment of new lordships and the construction of castles. Towards the Highlands and Islands are stone castles, such as Moulin or Dunstaffnage; around the semi-independent lordship or kingdom of Galloway the king established the lordships of the Bruces of Annan and others, with group of Flemings to the north in Lanarkshire. In the early 12th century Malcolm IV (or David I) gave them a series of small lordships along the upper Clyde; seven of the fifteen are now marked by mottes, and all by the establishment of village settlements. This was what lay behind the grants, the reorganization of the land to benefit from the nucleated pattern of fields and villages for the production of grain.

In Ireland some of the major castles, such as Trim and Ferns, were built close to earlier monastic sites which served as the main foci for settlement in the otherwise dispersed pattern of occupation of the Irish countryside, or, of course, the Norse towns, principally Dublin, Cork and Limerick. The great majority were founded on new sites, according to the needs of the new lords, sometimes military but much more often economic; the Carrickfergus of John de Courcy is a good example, a defensible site on a low rock promontory projecting into the sea, but principally chosen for its port and communications to John's estates inland (see **102**).

CASTLES IN MILITARY STRATEGY

There are examples of sites that demonstrate the use of a castle to defend land already taken. The valley of the river Seine links Paris and Rouen, the capitals of the kingdom of France and the Duchy of Normandy (see **72**). As such it was the scene of conflict between the king and the duke until 1204 when John, Duke of Normandy and King of England, lost his duchy to the King of France. His elder brother, Richard Coeur de Lion went on Crusade and was captured on his return by the Duke of Austria. Philip of France seized the opportunity to move the frontier from the line of the river Epte nearer Rouen. The river line had been heavily fortified with a chain of castles, like Gisors, but this was now useless to Richard. On his release from captivity he decided to establish a new line on the next tributary of the Seine, the Andelle, and crown the defences with a great new castle, Château Gaillard (see **96**). Here is a case of a new castle founded almost entirely as a military post, not to establish a

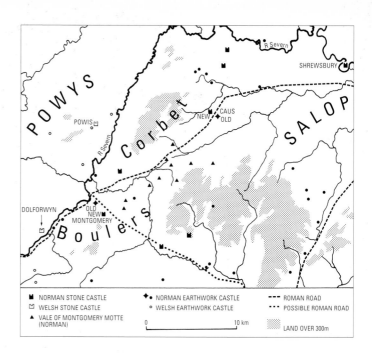

15 *(right)* The strategic positioning of castles; the mottes of his tenants in the Vale of Montgomery guarded by the Earl of Shrewsbury's castles at Hen Domen and Shrewsbury (after King & Spurgeon).

16 *(below)* Criccieth castle; a Welsh castle of the earlier 13th century added to by Edward I.

lordship but to defend it; it is interesting to note that its inner ward contains a splendid suite of rooms for the king's residence, whose arrangement conflicts with the defensive isolation of the keep as a point of last resort.

Castles more often appear in a defensive role as groups rather than as individuals. In the Vale of Montgomery we can see both the role of the individual castle and the one example where such a disposition seems to have been established (**15**). At the English end of the Vale lies Shrewsbury, the caput of the Earldom of Roger de Montgomery; at the Welsh end lay the major earthwork castle of Hen Domen. In between the similarity of the mottes allows us to suggest that they were the result of Roger requiring his tenants to build a 'standard' motte castle for their holdings. Hen Domen was replaced as a military strong point in the 1220s and 1230s by the stone castle of Montgomery. Its

17 *(above)* Totnes motte.

construction led to the Welsh prince Llywllyn ap Gruffydd building a stone castle, Dolforwyn, only 6km (4 miles) away.

The proliferation of castles in areas of military stress is well shown by the distribution of that most common form of simple castle, the earthwork motte, in the British Isles (**17**, **18**). They are thickest on the ground in Wales, especially along the English border. In Scotland they are rare in the eastern Lowlands, but commonest to the west, around Galloway; it is to these that the mottes of the Flemings of the upper Clyde belong. In Ireland, they are also unevenly distributed, sparse in the extreme south, but dense on the ground in the eastern Midlands and Ulster, around the major Irish kingdom of the O'Neills.

This concentration in areas of military tension can also work over time. Many of the smaller castles in England, principally mottes, appear to belong to the early 12th century rather than the late 11th, to the civil war under Stephen and Matilda rather than to the aftermath of 1066. If we can argue that mottes were rare in areas such as the eastern Lowlands of Scotland where the power of the king kept order, then we are entitled to propose that where mottes are relatively rare elsewhere, these areas or periods were also relatively free from war. This would include much of the south of Ireland, which on this evidence did not resist the English lordships much. It would also make one wonder how much the settlement of 1066 was opposed after the battle itself was over, outside the north and the Fens.

The principal lesson of all this is the equation of a castle and a lordship; the presence of a castle means that a lordship was once based there. A new castle implies a new lordship, and a new lordship needed a new castle. This continued throughout the Middle Ages. Edward II's cousin, the Earl of Lancaster wished to found a new centre in the north of England to consolidate his estates and power there; the result was the isolated castle of Dunstanburgh, started in 1313. In Yorkshire, Sir Henry Scrope founded the dynasty of the Lords Scrope in the later 14th century, while in south Wales in the next century Sir William ap Thomas (or Herbert) also founded a

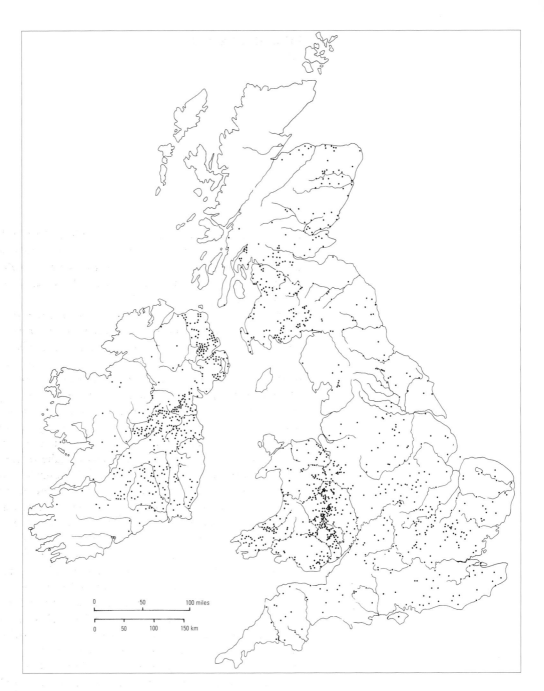

18 *(above)* Map of mottes in the British Isles.

new dynasty of lords. The results were the castles of Bolton and Raglan, respectively (see **49** and **53**). Sir William de Clinton celebrated his elevation to the Earldom of Huntingdon by building a new castle at Maxstoke away from the village, and giving the site of the earlier castle to a monastery.

HOW MUCH DID A CASTLE COST?

This brings us to the allied question of the costs of building castles; how big a commitment was a lord making when he embarked on the construction of a castle? In a sense, this is like asking the length of a piece of string, complicated by the fact that the costs which we do have recorded are given in pounds which are not just subject to the erosion of value through inflation since the Middle Ages, but whose purchasing power was different in the period. If, for example, the basic labourer's wage on a site is quoted as 1 or 2 pence per day (12 pence for a six day week), we must remember that there were 240 pence to the pound, and that this was take-home pay, with no tax or insurance deductions. We could produce a formula based on this daily wage rate and apply it as a multiplier to convert all 13th-century prices into a modern equivalent. The two pence might be equated reasonably with £40 in 2005 as daily take-home pay, giving 160 as the ratio between 13th-century money and modern. To apply this to all prices, or to wages of other groups of workers in the same ratio, however, would be quite wrong. They will not have varied in the same way; bread, for example, may well be proportionally cheaper now, while heavily taxed beer is certainly relatively dearer. The figures which we can quote of costs can only give a rough impression of their order of magnitude, related to the income of the lord concerned and to other commitments he might have had. Overwhelmingly, our evidence is derived from royal works, and we do not know how close these would have been to a baronial castle: they cannot have been very different, however.

It is possible to make a clear distinction between a castle of earth and timber and one of stone. It would take 50 people something in the order of 40 working days (of ten hours each) to pile up the earth for a 'basic' motte, 5m (16ft) high and 15m (49ft) across the top. A large motte, twice the height and 20m (66ft) across the top, would take a little over three times the effort. The earthworks of the bailey might require the same work as the motte. To this we would then have to add the work involved in erecting the timber structures, tower and palisade, plus the buildings of the bailey. The earthworks required no more than muscle power with some direction to stop men getting in each other's way when they dug out the earth or when they piled it up. The skills were purely those of organizing; the people of any agricultural community could be counted on to have the abilities, and most of the tools, needed for the basic earth moving. Nor need their labour have cost the lord money; we can imagine the arguments used to 'persuade' the peasants that they should work on a castle's earthworks. The only craftsmen required were the carpenters for the buildings; even here much of the woodwork, such as the palisade, would have needed little more than an axe and strong arms. It is unsurprising that the informal erection of timber castles has left little trace on the financial records of the Middle Ages. Timber and earth castles were also becoming rare just as the records that have come down to us were becoming common.

The medium-sized motte and bailey of Clones in Ireland was built as part of an unsuccessful attempt to expand the boundaries of the lordship of Meath to the north; it was probably not built by local peasantry conscripted for the purpose, because they would all have run away, but mostly by paid labour. It seems to have cost about £20 to build in 1211: over one half of this went on diggers, with a little more than a quarter on carpentry; this compares with a cost of just over £50 on the wages and supplies of the garrison and the cost of transporting them to the castle. It is also a good example of the failure of a castle alone to impose lordship on an area where the locals were hostile, for it was burned by the king of the neighbouring Cenel Eoghain after the English field army had left.

THE COSTS OF THE STONE CASTLES OF HENRY II

We may look at the costs of building stone castles by taking as examples two periods when their construction formed a major element of royal policy: the late 12th century under Henry II and his son Richard I; and the late 13th century under Edward I. Henry and his sons were much concerned with castles because control of them was a major element both in their wars in France and also in facing the rebellions that broke out in England. Edward was able to complete the conquest of north Wales by his field armies through the building of the magnificent series of castles there, which are rightly considered to be among the finest built in the Middle Ages. Both periods have left the documents that can supply the information we need to estimate cost. The main difference is that under Henry II and his sons the overall expenditure across the whole range of royal castles will be considered, many of which saw little significant building, while the reign of Edward I offers the chance to see the problems of building a set of new castles on 'green field' sites.

19 *(below)* Masons building a wall, as they showed themselves on a capital in Conques abbey, France.

20 *(above)* Orford castle tower, built at a cost of about £1400 by Henry II, over eight years.

The sums that Henry II and Richard spent varied greatly from castle to castle; not all were of equal importance to them and not all needed as much work. At one end are the castles, such as Exeter, Hereford or Gloucester, where expenditure rarely exceeded £50 in a year, and never exceeded £100; year after year sums in the order of £20 or £30 appear accounted for. This is significant in itself. Stone castles of the Middle Ages contained much timber, put in unseasoned; they rarely had a proper system of guttering for roofs, which were themselves of a variety of materials. Castles were in need of constant repair, hence the steady trickle of money needed just to keep them going. Aside from this came the constant theme of the periodic surveys on the state of the castle structures: 'ruinatum' (in need of repair); 'worth nothing beyond the costs of upkeep'.

Against these are the major works, which would also have varied both in the costs and the time taken. A simple small tower such as the one at Bridgnorth seems to have been built for less than £400; around £200 for the very small one at the Peak. The more complex examples at Scarborough (see **73**) or at Newcastle upon Tyne cost perhaps something like £500 or £1000 (the accounts include work on other parts of the castle too, without specifying precisely what) between 1167 and 1177. The castle at Orford was a new one, started in 1165–6 on a site with no existing buildings to use (**20**). By 1173 when new building apparently stopped, some £1400 had been spent, principally on the keep.

At the top end of cost-scales was the magnificent keep of Dover castle (see **29**), built at a cost of some £4000 between 1182 and 1187. This was only part of the estimated £6500–7000 spent on Dover castle between 1181 and 1191, £1300 in the year 1184–5; Richard spent £2400 on the Tower of London in one year, 1189–90. The most massive of the royal works of these years was the fortification of the river Seine on the new boundary of

Normandy, at Les Andelys, during the three years 1196 to 1198, which cost a little over £11,000 in the one year, 1198. It is unclear how much was spent in the other years, or how much was incurred in building the castle of Château Gaillard as opposed to the other fortifications (see **96**), but the figure for the latter must have been in the order of £15–20,000 in all. This was a castle with a keep and fine lodgings in the inner courtyard, itself one of three wards, all built of cut stone.

What do these figures mean in the context of their time? Henry II had a royal income from England alone (apart from Normandy, Anjou or Aquitaine) of something like £20,000 per annum. Much of this income was, of course, committed before it was collected to carrying on the business of the king and his household; the money spent on castles was not taken from £20,000 of freely available funds. Another way to express it would be to compare it with other costs. Richard I promised the Emperor of Germany £100,000 as ransom for his release after he was captured while returning from Crusade; not all of it was paid but a great amount was. A small army of 100 knights with 500 footmen would cost a little over £3500 to keep in the field for six months. Between the years 1177 and 1185, Henry II spent nearly £1200 on building works at the abbey of Waltham and £880 on the nunnery of Amesbury, an average of about £250 per year. This highlights the distinction between three groups: the few castles, like Dover, London or Château Gaillard, where truly massive sums were spent; the ones such as Orford and Newcastle which saw sums of around £1000 spent on them, and the rest which rarely cost more than £50 in a year. The first two groups give us an idea of the sort of commitment that the decision to erect a serious stone castle would call for. A minimum cost might be at least £1000, while building a first-rate castle in around 1200 would involve spending perhaps £10,000.

The costs of building were not all incurred in a single year. While an exceptional man, Richard I, when faced with the exceptional threat to the Norman frontier noted above, might bring about the construction of a first-rate castle at Château Gaillard in three years, this was by no means normal. Where there appears to have been no such exceptional pressure, there is some evidence to suggest that it might be usual to build a wall about 3–4m (10–12ft) higher each year; a great tower would thus take about eight or nine years to build. A man who proposed to construct a new castle, of reasonable, but not exceptional, strength in the years around 1200 would be committing himself perhaps to an average expenditure of something like £100 to £150 per year for ten years. There would be years of heavier expenditure in these as well as lighter ones. Clearly this is a load that the king of England could bear with ease; only the major castles would have caused him strain. To a baron, whose income might well not amount to £1000 per year, such a commitment was in quite a different order. It would mean devoting the entire income of two or three manors for a decade to the project. The contrast with the resources needed to put up a castle of earth and timber, such as Clones, is great. The later 12th century, when it became indispensable for a serious castle to be built of stone, marked a point after which castle building became simply too expensive for any but lords of more than a single manor to consider.

EDWARD I'S CASTLES IN WALES

The castles which Edward I built in north Wales formed part of his plans for the conquest of the country and its absorption into England. He fought three wars, in 1277, 1282–3 and 1293, with a lesser rising in 1287. Not all the castles were built at the same time: the first war resulted in the construction of Aberystwyth, Builth (in mid-Wales), Flint and Rhuddlan. The second war produced the castles of Caernarvon, Conway, Harlech and others; the revolt of 1294 resulted in the building of Beaumaris. Likewise the costs varied, from the relatively cheap additions to the pre-existing castles of Bere and Criccieth, where £265 and £318 respectively were spent, to the massive expenditure of some £14,500 at Beaumaris, or £19,900 on the castle and town walls of Caernarvon. The speed of work varied, too. Of the major castles, the town and castle of Flint were completed in a little over nine years at the approximate cost of £7000; Rhuddlan was completed in nine years (most of the work taking only four) for some £9000; Harlech (21) took some six years and £8000 to be substantially completed; Conway about five years and £14,000 for the great bulk of the work. Against these must be put the castles of Caernarvon, begun in 1283 and Beaumaris, begun in 1295, where work continued into the 1330s and yet still neither castle was even remotely finished.

21 *(above)* Harlech castle, built by Edward I in six years.

Like the figures for the castles of Henry II, we must try to put these costs into perspective. The whole programme of castle building in north Wales cost something in the order of £80,000 between 1277 and 1304, and a further £15,000 over the next 25 years. Edward's father spent just over £2000 a year on rebuilding Westminster Abbey for at least ten years, up to more than £40,000. In 1277 Edward undertook to build a new abbey at Vale Royal in Cheshire, and promised to spend £1000 a year on the works: in 1290 he lost interest, having spent about three quarters of the promised money. Between 1275 and 1306, Edward levied nine taxes on England, which were aimed at yielding totals of between £34,000 and £116,000 in a year, and which came near to doing so on occasions; their combined yields were aimed at over £500,000. In 1294 Edward formed an alliance with the princes of the Low Countries against France, promising them large subsidies: £40,000 to the King of the Germans, or £50,000 to the Duke of Brabant. The real contrast is with the cost of an army. For the defence of the Duchy of Gascony between 1294 and 1299, Edward spent over

£350,000 on armies in the field. The Welsh works, even the two castles of Caernarvon and Beaumaris, were clearly well within his capacity to pay and, compared with the expense of an army in Wales, they were an excellent investment at less than £10,000 in a year. It was not the cost of the Welsh works that led to his financial problems in the 1290s but the costs of his wars in general.

The costs that the king was able to bear with some equanimity were not so easy for others. Much of the work on the castle of Caerphilly in Glamorgan was apparently carried out in the twenty years before 1288; it was as ambitious as any of the works of Edward I in the north (see **8**). It was built by Gilbert de Clare, Earl of Gloucester, the richest baron of the time outside the royal family in England. Even he, however, must have found the cost of Caerphilly high, for it must surely have been in the order of £8–10,000; his annual income was about £6000.

THE BUILDERS

The survival of the detailed documents of the administration of the building of Edward's castles in Wales shows why the process was expensive. Two quotations from one letter sent by the man in charge of the building of Beaumaris, the great designer Master James of St George, to the Exchequer in Westminster tell the story:

> *In case you should wonder where so much money could go in a week, we would have you know that we have needed – and shall continue to need 400 masons, both cutters and layers, together with 2000 less skilled workmen, 100 carts, 60 wagons and 30 boats bringing stone and sea coal; 200 quarrymen; 30 smiths; and carpenters for putting in the joists and floor boards and other necessary jobs. All this takes no account of the garrison mentioned above, or of purchases of material, of which there will have to be a great quantity ... The men's pay has been and still is very much in arrears, and we are having the greatest difficulty in keeping them because they have simply nothing to live on.*

The numbers of men employed on the great works (especially because Edward was building several castles at once) were impressive: in 1277 when he started the first campaign of building,

22 *(below)* The upper gate of the town walls of Conway. The small square holes are for the scaffolding poles secured to the wall as it was built. They are arranged in a rising spiral, rather than in horizontal stages as scaffolding was in Savoy, where the master mason, Master James of St George, came from. The same scheme can be seen on the castle walls.

Edward recruited widely all over England. Almost 3000 men were gathered at Chester to go on to the works at Flint and Rhuddlan and elsewhere: these included 300 drainage workers from the fens of Lincolnshire, while Wiltshire, Somerset and Dorset contributed 120 carpenters and 120 masons (**19**). At their height, the works at Conway employed some 1500 men. They were recruited by the sheriffs of each of the counties involved and then walked to Wales. The work was to an extent seasonal; setting the stone and much of the unskilled digging were suspended during the winter months because of the weather and the short days, but the teams of skilled men were held together, working on preparing material for use in the next summer. Again we see the difference between the royal works and those of a baron. The king was able to call on the services of the county sheriffs for recruiting the men concerned, and he had a staff of experienced administrators, not only in the Exchequer but also because he was constantly commissioning building work. There was an international dimension to his operations that an individual baron would hardly be able to match. The chief masons involved in the Welsh works were, at the start Master Bertram from south-west France, and, for the greater part of the work, Master James of St George from alpine France (**22**).

At the ground level, when these many workmen had been recruited, their work needed to be co-ordinated. The stonework required a steady supply from the quarries, of the right type and size of stone; the masons had to cut it to the precise shape – even one layer of ordinary stones in a plain wall must all be of the same height – for the stone layers to assemble them in the walls. If any of these processes got out of balance, the others would be either behind in their work or have no work to do. The layers needed the scaffolding to rise up the walls with their work, the job of one of the branches of the carpenters.

The design of the timber roof and, to a lesser extent, the floors exerted a thrust on the stone walls, which had to be allowed for from the first. The master carpenter and the master mason must be agreed on this; later the floor joists had to be fitted into the walls at the right time: they must have been cut down in the forest and brought to the site in preparation for this, again a point of co-ordination between the carpenters and masons (**23**). Both skills need good tools; smiths had to be part of the operation to keep the others going, making and sharpening tools. The unskilled men had to be hired in sufficient numbers to bring the materials as they were needed, either to the site or around it, while the digging of ditches, particularly in wet ground, needs supervision: if this is not co-ordinated, access to the site could be cut off. It is no wonder that building a stone castle was expensive; it called for a lot of skilled men and good organization, which is never cheap.

CONCLUSION

If we look back at the building of an earthwork castle, the contrast is striking, not just in the cost, but in the complexity of the operations; even a large earthwork could be put up easily in one or two years, while a stone tower alone might be expected to take eight or ten. In military terms, it can be argued that building a castle should be a sound investment. The costs of maintaining an army in the field were such that if the much smaller garrison of a castle could hold up an invading force as well as an army, thanks to the strength of the castle fortifications, then the capital cost would be recouped. Of course, reducing a garrison's size reduced its cost, but it also reduced its capacity to damage the enemy by sallying out, unless it was reinforced in time of war. This meant either the king sending troops (which the castle was supposed to replace) or the garrison being reinforced by the local volunteer militia. This brings us back to the basic point of castles, that they were concerned with political control of the population, not with a purely military force; the locals could not be relied on to rally to their lord's defence automatically. These arguments only apply to a king; from the later 12th century the barons of England and the core of Scotland were not thinking of raising armies for independent action from their castles. It was only lords on the borders of feudal Britain, in Wales, Ireland or the Highlands of Scotland, that could entertain such thoughts. Yet castles continued to be built, by barons as well as kings.

In the 13th century even an Earl would have had to think twice before embarking on a new stone castle, while the idea would have been beyond the lord of an estate worth even £100 a year. This highlights the later 12th century as a crucial period in the development of castles. The rising costs of building, when stone replaced earth and timber in the minimum level of castle, drastically reduced the number of people who were able to pay for the building of castles. It should have made many people prefer to mend and make do with their old castles, rather than start to rebuild them on a large scale. Many did, for that is why castles of earlier periods survived, but there were still many new ones built. The cost that inhibited some spurred others on. Medieval aristocrats did not believe in being modest about their wealth and power. A lord who did not spend to the extent of his income soon forfeited the respect of his peers and his tenants. Castle building was an important element of the display of being a lord in the Middle Ages (**24**).

Castles were built to reinforce lordship or to establish a new lord in the possession of his lands. The effort that he put into his castles was considerable and analyzing it can tell us much of the priorities and intentions of the builder. This can be geographical: Henry II's relative lack of investment in the castles of the Welsh border has been seen as showing that his concern with this area was not a priority. A dense distribution of castles in time or space is an indication of military tension. The balance of the functions that a castle might perform tells us about the future role that its builder planned for it. The attention paid to defences and the provision for the household as an indicator of its size, are evidence both of the lord's lifestyle and of his view of his future needs. The changing role of castles reflected the changing patterns of lordship, as we will see in later chapters. These changes culminate in the ultimate change of role: abandoning the castle marked a real revolution in a European country.

23 *(above)* Timber centring and scaffolding supporting an arch under construction; this is the sort of work requiring close co-operation between mason and carpenter.

24 *(right)* Carved head of 14th-century style from Edlingham castle, dating from the rebuilding by Sir William Felton.

3 THE INNER HOUSEHOLD

The key requirement for a castle to be useful was that it should be a proper place for a lord to live and work in. Its heart was the accommodation of the lord and his household in the setting that he thought was right for the sort of life he wished to live, and be seen to live. Castles in this sense were very public places by modern standards: the millionaire recluse had no role in the medieval world. Ceremony was an essential cement to hold the grades of society together. A lord had to meet his tenants and supporters regularly and be seen to do so. He had to be seen both to mix with them graciously and consult them, while at the same time impressing them with his power. He had to do the same sort of thing with his equals and superiors. For this he needed a large impressive room, which could be reached formally by some sort of procession and where the people present could be arranged in their ranks. The grand hall of the old Germanic past, rectangular in shape, with an access end and a 'better' end for the lord to sit at was the core of this side of the castle. A lord and his agents organized his lordship from his castle and they needed the room to do it. As we have seen, these roles changed through time and the physical settings changed along with them. The lord's household became increasingly complex as it developed through the Middle Ages, and was composed of what might be termed successive concentric layers of people serving or dependent on him. All these people need rooms, either to sleep or to do business in. The castles we see now are only shells, without any of their internal furnishings, and usually without floors or roofs, and it is from these shells that we have to try to evoke life in them. As a first step we may take the inner core, the lord and his immediate associates.

RECONSTRUCTING THE USE OF BUILDINGS OR ROOMS

To understand the use of buildings, we must understand the features that tell us what an individual room was used for. We are looking for the differences between the types of public room – hall, kitchen or chapel, for example – and the distinctions in the private rooms that demonstrate the status of the men living in them within the hierarchy of the household as a whole. A room with good windows, a fireplace and access to a latrine can confidently be assumed to have been residential and for the use of the upper class of the castle population; a room with none of these is likely either to be a service room or for stores.

With the more strictly domestic rooms, we must note both the features they possess and their disposition within the complex. The hall forms the pivot between the service rooms and the domestic ranges, both literally and socially (see **36**, **62** and **100**). It is easy to identify; it is normally the largest structure in the castle, usually rectangular, and notable for its large windows (often with seats in recesses), fireplace in one wall, and access to latrines (usually more than one to cope with the numbers of people using the hall).

The grading system of the private rooms, the chambers, is similar: the better ones betraying themselves by better quality stone carving and size of both their windows (normally with seats) and their fireplaces. The private nature of a chamber is shown by its position and in the ease of access to it from public rooms such as the hall or chapel, or from the courtyard; also it should have a single latrine. In relation to the arrangement of rooms two things must be noted. They may be linked together themselves into suites, rather than being single units, and their relative position is also relevant. A room closer to the lord's chamber is more important than one remote from it, while the relationship to such features as the gatehouse, chapel or hall tells us something of its likely use. Unfortunately, no castle has survived with its wall coverings, whether painted plaster or woven hangings, and its furniture intact; both these things (and the style of the people within) played their part in the workings of the rooms, but we must supply them from other sources.

All this adds up to the fact that we can 'read' the accommodation provided in a castle, but only in certain ways. We can rank the rooms in status fairly reliably and we can distinguish between more 'private' rooms and public ones. We can note how some rooms are linked together by access, either from a stair or the courtyard, or to each other, and so consider that they were used together. Within this we may imagine that the ones further from the point of access were more private and, in modern terms, more exclusive. This may be a fallacy: medieval people did not value privacy in the same way as we do, neither as a thing to be desired, nor measured in the same way. The innermost room is as likely to be a private store as a bed chamber. Size, status and accessibility tell us a lot, but by no means everything. The castle of Chepstow gives us two examples, one positive and one negative, which show something of the problems. The first concerns the place of women in a castle. Clearly the Lady of a castle was important but it is surprisingly difficult to identify a suite of rooms in any castle which looks as though it was reserved for her. In this we must exclude the rooms lived in, or used, by a lady who was the mistress in her own right of the castle; here the rooms she occupies are simply the lord's ones occupied by his lady. The only help that contemporary literature is in giving any diagnostic feature of a lady's rooms is that they are likely to be associated with an enclosed (and private) garden. The west tower at the outer end of the Upper Bailey at Chepstow overlooks both it and the barbican beyond. By the late 12th century, when it was built, the western barbican and entrance were very definitely the 'back door' of the castle. It has been suggested that the barbican might well have acted as a garden and that the west tower might be the Countess' lodging. This is by no means self-evident (for example, it is difficult to tell if the barbican area was a garden, or a back yard) but what is interesting is that this is the only real candidate yet identified. There are subsidiary chambers off the lord's great chamber which have been described as his wife's but they could just as easily be those of confidential servants. The north-eastern range of Chepstow will be discussed later as an example of the planning of hall and lodgings. Here we may simply note that one of the principal rooms, the main eastern room, (see **35** and **36**) has been variously identified as a separate hall for guests, a kitchen and (here) as the Constable's hall for use when the lord was absent. If we can vary to this extent, clearly identifying the use of rooms and their occupants is not an exact science.

THE GREAT TOWERS OF THE 11TH AND 12TH CENTURIES

From their earliest forms, castles were different and the towers show it. Their image is that of the grim 'keep', essentially a military stronghold, but their details do not bear this out. One of the earliest is the tower of Loches, built for the Counts of Anjou in the 1020s and 1030s. It combines the two core functions of the castle. It is entered on the first floor where there is a great hall, with access and passages to kitchens outside; the food could be served with ceremony, even if it was cold as a result. Above this are other rooms, heated with fireplaces in the walls, presumably accommodation for the Count and his officers. Combining the ceremonial hall with the living accommodation for the lord was a continuing theme through to the end of the 12th century. At Richmond Alan the Red, or his brothers, built the present stone enclosure castle before 1100 (**25**, **27**). At the south-east angle he built his hall with a single chamber for himself, both at first-floor level. Two great towers in Kent show the earliest signs of complexity: Rochester built from 1127 onwards (see **74**) and Canterbury probably a little earlier. Again, in common with the majority of great towers, they are entered at first-floor level. The ground floor in nearly all great towers functioned as a basement, usually confined to storage (often we will be passing over this level, as well as the roof top which played a purely military role). At Canterbury, the tower is much ruined but we can see something of its layout. It was divided into three sections: there was

25 *(below)* A reconstruction of Richmond castle as it may have looked in c.1100. The hall and chamber can be found in the building at the top of the enclosure.

26 *(right)* Aerial view of Castle Rising; the decorated entry stair faces across at the entrance into the great earthwork enclosure.

a hall in the centre, reached directly from the outside. On one side of the hall was a kitchen and another room, of similar size but equipped with a wall chamber; and on the other side a large room with a fireplace and access, via a spiral stair, to the other floors and a small room beside it. It is tempting to see this arrangement as a hall, a kitchen and chapel on the one side and a chamber with a private one off it on the other. Be that as it may, there was a second floor that must have provided further accommodation. At Rochester, the hall occupies the second floor, along with the chapel, both being reached from the same, main, stair. Off the hall are small chambers in the thickness of the walls. Both the first and third floors have a pair of main rooms, each with fireplaces, occupying the central space of the tower, while the third floor also has a number of lesser chambers in the walls, like the hall below. Hesitantly (partly because of the poor preservation of the tower) at Canterbury, but more confidently at Rochester, we can see two ideas being developed. One is the double chamber; the outer chamber for daytime life perhaps, and the other a small, sleeping room. The second idea is that of providing separate rooms for others than the lord; presumably these were for the upper members of his household.

King Henry II built Orford castle between 1165 and 1173 (see **20**). The entry leads into a hall, off which open doors to a kitchen and a small private chamber. The floor above is the main one, with a large hall, also with a kitchen and a private chamber. In a mezzanine floor between the first and second ones is the chapel, linked to a chamber that was presumably for the chaplain. The contemporary great tower at Newcastle upon Tyne contains the main elements, hall, chapel and chamber, and also provides separate rooms for others than the lord. On the one hand we can identify the chaplain's room, but also, most clearly at Newcastle, a second, inner suite of rooms that may be for the queen; it was not entered directly from the outside. In all three cases mentioned above, the household was accommodated in the one tower, living, if not in the same room as in the early 12th century, at least all together.

27 *(above)* The hall and chamber of Richmond Castle; the simple living provision of a late 11th-century castle.

If some towers appear to combine the main elements of public and private life into the one building, others are specialized and provide for only one or the other. Some are almost entirely for public ceremonial. The Tower of London remains as a splendid monument to the power of William the Conqueror. As with most great towers a visitor entered at first-floor level – into a large room with a fireplace in one wall, while off this were two other rooms. The main floor was above, marked out as the principal one by being twice the height. It had only three rooms: the chapel, a large hall over the entry room below and a room backing on to the chapel. This has been interpreted as a throne room, with the hall for even more ceremonial events. There is no small living room and a kitchen is conspicuously absent. The great tower of Chepstow, built by William fitz Osbern in the 1060s, continued a tradition of 10th- and 11th-century French castles (as does the Tower of London) and consisted of a single strong rectangular stone building, with a hall occupying two-thirds of the main floor area. Two rooms occupied the remaining third of the building, one over the other.

Castle Rising tower was built by William de Albini to celebrate his political and social coup of marrying Henry I's widow and its arrangements are elaborately designed for ceremony. The tower presents its most elaborately decorated face towards the entrance into the castle enclosure (**26** and see **11**). The decoration is concentrated on the outside of the wide entry stair which leads to an unheated waiting room at the top. After being permitted to proceed, or welcomed in, the visitor could go on into the hall, distinguished by a wide niche in the long wall, perhaps the seat of William's ceremonial chair (or throne). The same is seen at Hedingham, also built to celebrate the rise of a family, the De Veres,

28 *(below)* Floor plans of the great tower at Dover castle.

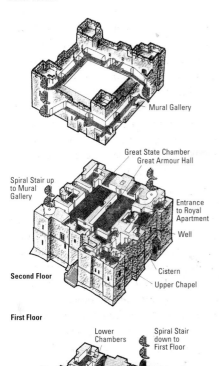

Mural Gallery

Great State Chamber
Great Armour Hall

Spiral Stair up
to Mural
Gallery

Entrance
to Royal
Apartment

Well

Cistern

Upper Chapel

Second Floor

First Floor

Lower
Chambers

Spiral Stair
down to
First Floor

Lower Hall
(Waterloo Model)

to power and the Earldom of Oxford. It has only two rooms over a basement: an entry room on the first floor and a grand hall above, distinguished by a magnificent arch over it and equipped with a gallery from which to watch the ceremonies below. At Dover (built by Henry II in the 1180s) the entry is at second-floor level, leading into the hall (**28, 29**). At the same level are the chapel, again with a chaplain's chamber, and a large chamber, off which lies a small room, only later equipped with a fireplace; this is barely large enough for a bed. While the hall, intended for use by many people, has a two-person latrine, the chamber has a single one, showing its more private nature, such as a small office. It also communicates directly with the chapel, appropriate to the clerical staff of the King. Below (on the first floor) the pattern is largely repeated, as it is, perhaps surprisingly, on the ground floor.

These towers were not meant to be lived in; we know that Henry II had a 'house' for this within the enclosure of Dover; he went into the great tower only on grand occasions. In all these we can imagine the opportunities for a procession or greeting of ceremony. The lord could greet his guest at the gate of the castle, at the foot of the stairs to the tower, at the entry to the hall, or at his seat according to the honour he wished to show. Equally, the guest could be asked to wait, or even be humiliated at each stage, especially if in times past he had been ushered through.

There are towers which are the mirror image of the ceremonial ones, dedicated to the lord's accommodation alone. The great tower at Conisbrough castle is not precisely dated, although it is usually attributed to Henry II's half-brother at the end of the 12th century. It provided two large rooms on the floors above the entry, both with fine fireplaces and single latrines. The upper of these, at third-floor level, has a chapel attached to it. The tower seems to be designed to provide a plain entry room, a great chamber on the second floor and a private chamber with chapel on the floor above. The foundations of the great hall, excavated in the courtyard, are more or less contemporary. The tower appears to be for the lord and his inner household, away from the general public life of the castle.

King John built a new suite of rooms for himself, the Gloriette, in the inner courtyard beside the old great tower of his castle at Corfe in the first decade of the 13th century. As so often, the building mainly functions at first-floor level, reached by a stair and

29 *(right)* View of the great tower at Dover castle.

30 *(below)* The floor plan of the great tower at Trim, Co. Meath; compared with Dover, the rooms are arranged in a more complex pattern to give a private suite on the second floor and the lord's great chamber on the third. The arrows mark the route from the entrance to the most private room on the second floor.

THE INNER HOUSEHOLD

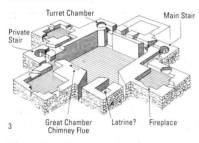

Turret Chamber   Main Stair
Private Stair
3   Great Chamber   Latrine?   Fireplace
Chimney Flue

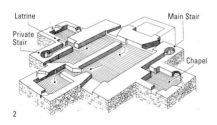

Latrine   Main Stair
Private Stair
Chapel
2

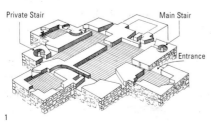

Private Stair   Main Stair
Entrance
1

through a formal porch. A hall, or great chamber, opened off the porch; at one end of the hall was a small but elaborate room, identified as a presence chamber but equally possibly a chamber for a key official, while at the other end was another chamber running off at a right angle. This was apparently the king's private chamber, while there was seemingly a second pair of chambers later allocated to the queen.

1169 saw the beginning of the establishment of English lordships in Ireland. The new lords needed castles to live in proper state at the head of their new estates. At Nenagh, Theobald Walter followed and improved on the example of William Marshal at Pembroke in the 1190s and built a round tower separated from the hall: his was noticeably more comfortable and well decorated than Marshal's, however, and clearly meant for his private tower. At Carrickfergus in the 1180s John de Courcy of Ulster put up a great square tower, which is remarkable because it does not contain either the castle's great hall, or a chapel; instead it seems designed purely for the accommodation of John and his household. The great tower and castle of Trim stand at the head of the Irish castles (**30**, **32**). There too the tower does not include the hall, which is some way across the courtyard, but it does include a chapel. This is situated for easy general access, down a passage from the main stair which leads up to the lord's great chamber on the third floor: mural passages above this room lead to four lesser chambers. The tower has two stairs; one reached directly from the entrance, the other

31 *(above)* A reconstruction of the courtyard castle at Old Sarum.

32 *(below)* View of the great tower at Trim castle.

more private. The two stairs make it possible to vary the accessibility of different rooms in a complicated system of circulation, which also links together some rooms into suites and not just undifferentiated chambers.

It might be argued that in these castles the accommodation was constrained by the demands of the site or because it was all to be contained within a tower. Richmond castle is remarkable because the hall and chamber block is set at the angle of a large enclosure. There were other courtyard castles in the 12th century where we can see the inner accommodation unconfined to a tower. Roger, the great minister of Henry I and Bishop of Sarum, built the castle of Sherborne in the first quarter of the 12th century as a courtyard set within a larger enclosure. There is a hall on one side with a chapel on the first floor of the other. In the angle at one end of the hall is a tower, not freestanding but attached to the two ranges beside it. This seems to have been for the Bishop and his immediate household, with further accommodation in the range between it and the chapel. He also occupied a similar courtyard house at Sarum itself (**31**) and his rival Henry of Blois built a more magnificent courtyard at his palace at Winchester. Bishops needed accommodation, not for their families (although Roger was notorious for the existence of his children in spite of being a bishop) but for their households, which were swollen by the number of administrative clerks. In spite of this, and with a courtyard plan able to provide any amount of space, the accommodation is, in fact, quite limited. Few people in the household seem to have anything resembling private rooms in the modern sense, with a lot of them sleeping communally.

In the early 13th century the Archbishop at Canterbury, and the bishops of Wells and Lincoln, had stone blocks at the core of their palaces. On each of the two floors there is a hall and a chamber, with a latrine serving the latter. In the latest, at Wells built in the 1230s, a gallery flanks the hall, and there is an inner chamber off the main one. Again, however, as in the royal castles, the bishop appears to put little space between his own room, or rooms, and the rooms for his household.

These castles of the years around 1200 give us the basis for all the later domestic planning of the Middle Ages. The lord's private accommodation, which began to be demarcated in the later 12th-century great towers, is now built physically separate from the great hall and the most public part of the castle's social life. At the same time the lord is no longer content with a single chamber but now lives in at least a pair of rooms. His household, likewise, is no longer prepared to share one or two undifferentiated rooms: we can see the growth of a hierarchy of rooms, distinguished by their size, their decoration and equipment, and by their placing in relation to the lord's chamber. At Trim, and perhaps at Corfe, we can see these also linked into pairs of rooms. The days of camaraderie when the lord and his men bedded down more or less together in a few rooms in a single great tower or other building were gone. The accommodation provided for the lord was now a separate part of the castle, and so increasingly were the rooms of his chief officers. Both were steadily developed during the 13th century.

THE PROLIFERATION OF CHAMBERS

At Barnard Castle it may have been John de Baliol who celebrated his acquisition of an heiress and estates in the 1230s by building both a new great hall, with service rooms and kitchen at the one end, and a great round tower for his own accommodation beyond an outer great chamber at the other (**33, 34**). At other castles we can see this arrangement preserved for what it was: the centrepiece of a complex of other rooms for members of the lord's household. At Ludgershall and at Clarendon, both hunting lodges for Henry III in

33 *(above)* A reconstruction of the inner ward of Barnard castle in the 13th century, with the great chamber and round tower attached to the great hall.

the forests of Wiltshire, the 13th century saw the addition of individual chambers, or pairs of chambers, to the nucleus of the hall and king's great and private chamber; these are known to have been added for the queen and for Lord Edward, the king's son and heir, but there are others for other members of the royal household. At both these places, and particularly at Clarendon, the buildings were able to sprawl across the site, creating more than one loosely defined courtyard; at Ludgershall they obliterated the earlier castle defences. At Sandal castle when Earl Warenne rebuilt the earlier wooden castle buildings around the courtyard in stone, he respected the earlier line of the defences, so that his range of buildings curved round in a semicircle within it. He built a hall with services at the one end, and then continued the line with a pair of chambers (outer and inner). These were not his own lodgings, for his were on the top of the old motte, but for his steward or the constable of the castle; they linked up with the main gatehouse of the castle.

Two castles of the Welsh border show the problems posed to the designer by the need to fit the complex of rooms that later 13th-century households demanded into existing walls. At Ludlow the great hall sits in the centre of two blocks (see **100**). To the west, the three doors indicate the presence of the service rooms at ground floor: above them on the first floor is a large chamber, with a separate, smaller one on the second floor; the two are only linked by being reached from the same stair which leads up from the hall. At the east end, at the level of the hall, is a pair of chambers, inner and outer. Over this is another great chamber, with an inner room off it; a stair leading up from the door between the two goes to a second inner chamber on the floor above. East of this again was a third block containing pairs of chambers: at the hall level they seem to have been of similar size to those just described, but above this the inner chambers at least were clearly smaller.

At Chepstow Roger Bigod celebrated his acquiring control of the lordship by rebuilding the domestic accommodation in the lower bailey, at the east of the castle (**35**, **36**). The arrangement involved fitting the range of buildings into a site that sloped down from west to east. There were two halls, the west one both bigger and better decorated; it has a set of chambers in a tower to the west. The designer exploited the fall of slope on the site by combining the service rooms of the two halls, with those serving the west hall on

34 *(right)* Air view of the inner court of Barnard castle under excavation, showing the foundations of the hall and the service chambers at the end away from the round chamber tower.

35 *(below)* The complex planning of the two halls and the attached chambers as built by Roger Bigod in the late 13th century at Chepstow castle. The great hall is at a higher level than the lesser one, because of a slope on which the block is built, which allows the one service passage to serve both halls.

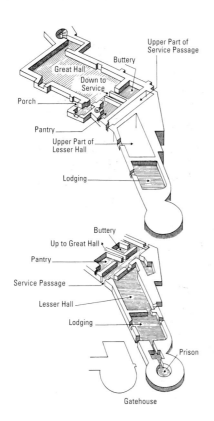

Upper Part of Service Passage

Buttery

Great Hall

Down to Service

Porch

Pantry

Upper Part of Lesser Hall

Lodging

Buttery

Up to Great Hall

Pantry

Service Passage

Lesser Hall

Lodging

Prison

Gatehouse

the floor above those of the east (or smaller) hall, identified as a hall by its traceried window and service rooms, although it has also been called a kitchen, in spite of lacking a large, original fireplace. Above the west hall service rooms is another single large chamber. East of the east hall is another set of chambers, linked to the earlier gatehouse of the castle; the rooms in a gatehouse were often the lodgings of the Constable of the castle (to watch the gate). The hall could be linked to these, as they are at Goodrich, and be a lesser hall for the Constable, permanently resident in the castle to hold courts in the name of the lord when he was absent. Across the courtyard Bigod built a massive tower (Marten's tower) that provided a guard room at entry level with two floors above, an outer chamber and a private chamber with a small but elaborate private chapel.

In these major castles, the arrangements of the living rooms conform to a general pattern. The hall is paramount and its position reflects this. A number of chambers were now to be found within castles providing accommodation for the important members of the lord's household, either his relatives or his officers. Among these rooms, we can begin to see specific associations emerging during the later 13th century.

It was primarily defence which called for the development of the gatehouse, but it also lent itself to providing a suite of linked rooms. These became quickly connected with the constable of the castle, the officer who permanently lived there, even when the lord

36 *(above)* View of Roger Bigod's hall range at Chepstow, from the top of his private chamber tower; the great hall is to the left, the lesser hall (or kitchen) to the right between it and the gatehouse.

37 *(right)* Reconstruction view of the gate passage with the constable's lodging over it, at Goodrich castle.

was absent, and who was responsible for its security; the gate was clearly the right place for him to live in and control (**37** and see **42**). The portcullis was difficult to combine with living. It had to rise up into the room over the gate passage, taking up space. To raise it the men needed a windlass with counterweights; this machinery also took up space, possibly in an upper, or attic, space. Possibly the presence of the portcullis mechanism in his chamber served as a symbol of the Constable's power and responsibility.

The need for courts and business to go on even though the lord was away for long periods seems to have led to the existence in some castles of a lesser hall (as suggested here at Chepstow) where the lord's officer could preside in less state than the lord in the great hall. Over the service rooms of the hall was often built a large chamber, which by its position would be appropriate for the chamberlain to use. The separation of rooms, and their functions within the inner household, is the physical reflection of the expansion and regularization of the household organization that the documentary evidence shows as happening by the middle of the 13th century. The popularity of mural towers in 13th-century designs, traditionally attributed to the needs of defence, may in fact be as much about providing rooms (see **5**). It was common for them to have a number of rooms, one on each floor, with a fireplace and latrine. These were all accessed from a single stair but otherwise separate and served as a block of rooms for members of the household. It is against this background that it is remarkable, and regrettable, that we cannot identify commonly, or with any confidence, rooms for the lord's wife and children, either as individuals or as a group; the wife and her attendants, the children's nursery. The overall scheme was still architecturally haphazard in that the common elements seem to have been arranged together in no particular order in the examples we have discussed. The care taken to fit them into a single overall scheme for the whole castle appears to happen later.

The castles discussed were built by the king or by major lords. As we saw, the rising costs of stone building in the 12th century caused many men to drop out of the castle-building race. Costs continued to rise in the 13th century, and stone-built houses emerge which are not in any real sense castles but are country houses. In their domestic planning, they, like royal hunting lodges or bishops' palaces, conformed in some way to the domestic planning ideals of the larger castles. At Temple Manor, Rochester or Moigne Court, the house is a simple hall and chamber on the first floor over a vaulted ground floor. These are the stone cores of manor houses, in the case of Moigne Court still partly surrounded by a moat; Penhallam manor is an excavated example of the same thing, a hall and chamber apparently with no other provision for the manor lord. Old Soar manor also had a hall with two chambers at one end, the one above the other, with the first-floor one linking to a chapel. In the west Highlands of Scotland, among Gaelic lords whose power was not based on feudal organization, the MacDougall lord had a hall and chamber tower by the end of the 13th century inside his castle at Dunstaffnage, which was too small to have provided much else in the way of lodgings.

Significantly there are places where later lords added chamber towers for themselves in addition to the earlier accommodation. At Stokesay (see **50**) at the end of the 13th century when the rich wool merchant, Lawrence de Ludlow, bought the manor, he built an outer and inner chamber in a separate tower for himself. Around 1300 Robert Thorpe, steward of the abbey of Peterborough, added the chamber tower to the hall at Longthorpe; the hall has now gone but the tower, with its contemporary wall paintings, survives (**39**). The late 13th century also saw Bishop Burnell, Chancellor of England build a castle at his ancestral home at Acton Burnell. This now consists of a single block with a lesser hall and chamber on the ground floor, and his own hall and chambers on the floor above; doors in the east wall show that it was linked to service rooms now gone. A smaller tower nearby is Hopton, which Walter de Hopton built to give himself a great and private chamber over a lesser one on the ground floor. At Edlingham in the 14th century Sir William Felton added a similar chamber tower, with two vaulted floors for himself, to the hall and chamber that he had inherited (**38** and see **7**). These are all scaled-down versions of the greater castle arrangements. The difference is the provision, not for the lord but for his household. County gentry and Highland lords did not have to accommodate the same size of household as a major lord of the feudal world.

These castles, great and small, are examples of the survival of the prestige of the great tower. While it might have been less important as a military feature, the idea of a tower as being a proper place for the lord's own lodgings continued: it was there at Chepstow, with

38 *(above)* Edlingham castle, where Sir William de Felton added a tower for his chamber to the earlier hall (seen here across the courtyard) of his manor house.

39 *(below)* The chamber in the tower of Longthorpe castle. The tower belongs to a manor house, but the paintings are a unique survival of the decoration of a medieval chamber; a great lord's castle would have been much richer.

Marten's tower. It can be seen at its most elaborate (not to say theatrical) at John de Warenne's Sandal castle. Here the great hall and the main lodgings were in the bailey of the old motte and bailey. John not only built a tower on top of the motte, unfortunately demolished in the 17th century, but provided it with a separate barbican which formed a ceremonial entrance to it from the bailey. It led to a narrow passage between two towers and then up the motte to the Earl's lodgings. It is easy to see the possibilities for ceremony here: trumpets announcing his departure from the tower, his arrival in the barbican tower, his crossing the bridge to the bailey and then his actual entry into the hall. Equally the tower on the motte imposed both the castle itself and also the power of its lord on the countryside around.

Even in newly built castles of the last quarter of the 13th century, where the opportunity existed to provide a fresh and coherent plan to the whole castle, without needing to have regard to earlier curtain walls or buildings, there are haphazard plans. Caerphilly, built in the years after 1270 by the Earl of Gloucester, the richest layman in Britain outside the royal family, and a superb example of the latest military thinking, had a hall against one side of the inner curtain and lodgings distributed through the towers without any apparent conscious planning (see **8**). Denbigh castle was started after 1282 by Henry de Lacy, Earl of Lincoln, as part of Edward I's conquest of north Wales; like Caerphilly it is a fine example of a major military castle of the time. Its kitchen, hall, and lord's chambers are simply accommodated within wall towers or sited against the curtain wall in a line: there is no attempt to make them

40 *(above)* Aerial view of Caerlaverock castle. A formal architectural plan of c.1277 much rebuilt later.

interrelate or to link them into a single unit of building. In these, as with the other examples discussed above, the castle fortifications are the first priority and the other buildings are fitted in afterwards.

THE GROWTH OF CONSCIOUS PLANNING AND DESIGN

Caerlaverock was rebuilt around 1277 on a new site (40). It was built to a remarkable plan, triangular (or, in the words of the poem describing its siege in 1300, shield-shaped), with the gatehouse at the apex. It is an awkward design (it is difficult to build rooms at the corners) and clearly a deliberate conceit.

The internal buildings and planning have not always survived well at Edward I's castles in Wales. The most elaborate and best preserved is Conway, built in the main in the five years from 1283, and certainly one of the castles where Edward I stayed (40a, 41). The castle is interesting from the aspect of planning, not least because here was a difficult site, along a narrow ridge, and one that did not make for ease in designing an integrated courtyard plan. Master James of St George solved this problem by dividing the castle into two courtyards by a strong wall. The main gate at the end of the castle led into the outer ward; a range with a chapel, a lesser hall and a chamber took up most of one long side; connected to it was the prison tower, so that it seems reasonable to identify this as a Constable's accommodation. The kitchen and service range was opposite, with stores.

The inner ward was given over to the king's apartments on the first floor, with rooms (equipped with latrines and fireplaces) for his

40a *(above)* Aerial view of Conwy castle. The castle entrance is to the bottom, leading to the outer court; the inner court lies beyond the cross wall.

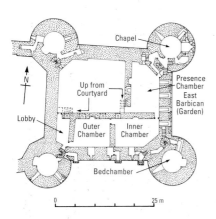

41 *(above)* Plan of the king's apartments on the first floor of the inner ward at Conway castle.

principal officials on the ground floor. There were two entrances to the king's suite from the courtyard below, both leading to outer chambers, which are set against the south and east walls of the inner courtyard, one of which is rather larger and better decorated with fine window tracery. This must have been the Presence Chamber, the principal public room for Councils to be held and distinguished visitors greeted: the smaller one would be for more private business and it is perhaps significant that there is a lobby outside it for visitors to wait in. The larger outer chamber is also linked to the private chapel, again a convenience for ceremonial. Behind both outer chambers lies the king's inner chamber, in the angle of the courtyard, so that it can have doors to both outer chambers.

The tower at the actual angle of the castle houses bedchambers on two floors, reached from the inner chamber, presumably for the king and queen. A final touch is that there is a stair leading directly from the inner chamber to the east barbican, which was used for a private garden, and thence to a small private gate to the castle. Two aspects are striking. There is the careful division of the castle into the public outer ward and the inner, private one. Within this the rooms are carefully arranged in a coherent suite, not only providing outer and inner chambers, but placing them in the castle in such a way as to make it easy to arrange their linking doors in the right sequence. This is not planning by accretion of the various parts, but is instead a systematic design from the first.

Either William de Valence, who died in 1296, or his son, Aymer, who died in 1324, was responsible for the building of the Goodrich castle that we see today (**42, 43**). It is more or less square in overall plan and most carefully arranged, in this case with four ranges around a single courtyard. The gatehouse is in the north-east angle, while the great hall is distinguished by its size and windows and is sited across the court against the west curtain wall. The hall is the pivot, not just socially, but also in the whole physical planning. It is clearly oriented with the upper, lord's end to the north and the service rooms to the south (with a chamber over them) and the kitchen built against the south curtain wall; the hall fireplace is not quite central but set nearer the lord's end. North of the hall is an entrance lobby (with benches for the waiting visitor) separating it from the lord's suite set against the north curtain wall and including the north-west tower. The suite consisted of a large

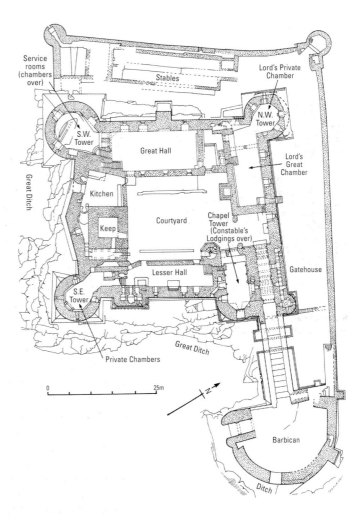

42 *(right)* Plan of the major rooms at Goodrich castle.

outer chamber at ground-floor level with an inner chamber in the north-west tower. At first-floor level, reached by a stair from the great chamber are two private chambers, while there is a pair of rooms at basement level below the great chamber and the north-west tower, reached by a stair from the lobby; a small door leads out from the larger one into the outer ward. The basement rooms must be for servants (there is no fireplace in the larger of the two basement rooms) close to de Valence, whose bedchamber was on the first floor with his wife's.

The east range provided a lesser hall that connected with a series of individual rooms in the south-east tower and to the lodgings at first-floor level in the gatehouse: the chapel was in the ground floor of the gatehouse. This repeats the planning of Chepstow where

43 *(above)* Aerial view of Goodrich castle. The hall range is along the near side; the gatehouse is to the upper left, with the barbican beyond it.

there was also a lesser hall; these have been described as for visitors and their households. Visitors themselves, if they were of the rank to have a large travelling household, would have dined with de Valence at high table in the great hall. The connection with the gatehouse lodgings, the normal seat of the constable, makes it more likely that these lesser halls were for the constable and the reduced household to use for courts in the absence of the lord.

THE LATER 14TH-CENTURY CASTLES

The successful captains of the Hundred Years War (1337–1453) have left us a number of fine castles, from the later 14th century in particular. Kenilworth is an interesting example from the 1380s and 1390s, when John of Gaunt decided to rebuild the accommodation within the confines of the earlier curtain wall. The result was rather like a 13th-century haphazard plan in that it was a semicircle of buildings around the courtyard from the kitchen to the chapel (**44**). There, however, the similarity ends, for Kenilworth is extremely carefully laid out, to provide a magnificent ceremonial setting for his state. The hall lies in the centre of the semicircle, with service rooms and kitchen lying to the north. South-east of the hall are a lobby, a presence chamber, a second lobby, an inner chamber, a private chamber (poorly preserved) and then the chapel. The lobbies are triangular in plan, which overcomes the problem of putting rectangular buildings around a semicircle. The junctions

44 *(above)* Aerial view of Kenilworth castle. The great hall is at the left of the inner crescent of buildings; the dam (used as a tiltyard) is at the bottom of the picture. A broad white path runs along its top.

between the hall, presence chamber and inner chamber are marked on the courtyard side by octagonal turrets.

The finest architectural effect is reserved for the outer facade of the hall range. The hall itself is conspicuous with its wide traceried windows. On either side are wide, shallow rectangular towers defined by small hexagonal turrets, which appear to be placed symmetrically at either end of the hall. In fact they are not: while the tower at the service end does mark the end of the hall, at the upper end the hall projects half way into the interior of the tower space. The two towers are also quite different in their architectural treatment: the one at the lower end of the hall is plain with narrow windows, as opposed to the tracery in the windows of the tower at the upper end. There could be no doubt in the mind of anyone looking at the inner or the outer facades of this range as to where John of Gaunt lived or as to his power. Like Goodrich, but not Conway, the design incorporates the great hall as the centrepiece of the planning by formalizing and making overt the distinction between its upper and lower ends.

Sir Edward Dalyngrigge, a knight with fewer resources than John of Gaunt, erected Bodiam castle at very much the same time as Kenilworth. It was built from new in a formal square plan, which allowed the internal planning to be laid out according to a symmetrical scheme. The castle divides along the line from the main gate in the north to the entrance to the great hall, through which lies a smaller postern gate, to the south. East of this line lies the great hall, with its upper end (lit by a window to the outside of the castle as well as the windows, now destroyed, which must have opened to the courtyard), Sir Edward's lodgings and the chapel. To the west of the line were the services and kitchen at the lower end of the hall, with a chamber in the south-west tower. The north-western quadrant of the castle has largely been destroyed but the narrow windows show that it was of lower status than the eastern range. Dalyngrigge's suite, on the first floor, was entered from the hall through a lobby and consisted of a presence chamber and an inner chamber, with two bedchambers off it: the inner chamber also connected to his private pew in the chapel. A similar range of rooms on the ground floor provides a parallel suite for an important official (it lacks the lobby from the great hall, one of the bedchambers and the private pew). Between the chapel and the gatehouse lies a lesser hall on the first floor, with a chamber in the north-east tower, which linked to the suite of rooms over the gate; the whole over the ground-floor rooms. Again this lesser hall may be suggested as for the permanent staff of the castle when the lord was away. The symmetry of the design is as striking as the facade of Kenilworth, but it is interesting to see that it was not rigorously carried through. Not only are the internal arrangements not the same on both sides of the line, but also the differences were displayed on the outside of the castle. The hall in particular, and Dalyngrigge's lodgings, were overtly signalled in the wider windows opening to the exterior. Some have suggested that these windows jeopardized the military strength of the whole castle, but clearly Dalyngrigge was as much interested in displaying his position, both in society and within the castle, as in strict military concerns.

The 14th century saw the Percies rise to great power as Earls of Northumberland, and they celebrated it at Warkworth at the end of the century. The castle culminates in a great tower carried on the early motte, emblazoned with a massive Percy lion facing over the town below (**45, 47, 48**). This tower provided a magnificent self-contained residence for the Earl. The entry was at ground-floor level, although the rest of the floor was largely taken up with storage rooms; there is an element of theatricality here in the contrast between the dark doorway and stair and the size and light of the rooms on the first floor. On the first floor was a hall, with a kitchen and service rooms at one end, and a chapel and outer chamber at the other. Above the outer chamber lay the inner one with a bedchamber; the inner chamber connected with galleries over part

45 *(below)* The Lion of the Percies carved on the lord's great tower (over his chamber) facing down to the town.

46 *(right)* Floor plans of Bolton castle. The late 14th century saw the development of very complex plans to incorporate the many sets of rooms into the overall plan of the castle, here a formal square *(Archaeological Journal)*.

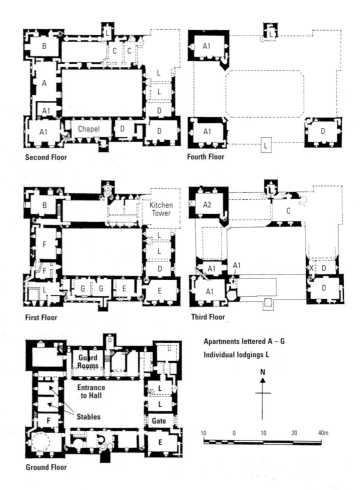

of the chapel and the hall. This tower was in addition to the great hall and large chapel in the courtyard of the castle, while there were further lodgings in the towers found along the curtain walls.

At the same time as the Percies were building Warkworth, another family which had risen to power in the north of England, the Scropes, were displaying their position in a new castle at Bolton (**49**). Again, we have a very formal design for the whole castle, a symmetrical rectangle like Bodiam, but with square towers and a much more restricted courtyard in the middle (**46**). The north front of the castle was largely taken up with the great hall on the first floor, while the chapel occupied the western half of the south range, on the second floor. Between these two public areas, in the western range, were Lord Scrope's lodgings, set up on the second floor. They were reached from the upper end of the great hall

47 *(above)* Air view of Warkworth castle (see also figure 65).

through a lobby set between the lodgings of two officers. The whole castle provides a carefully graded circuit from the great hall, leading in one direction to the elaborate apartments of the lord and the suites of his main officers and to the kitchen in the other. Just as carefully as the buildings of a monastery were set around the cloister and graded by their proximity to the east end of the church, so too were the rooms of Goodrich, Bodiam or Bolton castles, in relation to the two ends of the great hall and the inner chamber of the lord.

The same organized circuit of lodgings around a tight courtyard can be seen at Wardour, except that it is built not in a rectangle but a hexagon. The great hall is set over the main entrance, rebuilt in the early 17th century but surely originally designed for the sort of heraldic sculpture as the Percy lion at Warkworth. The hexagon of Wardour, and the triangle of Caerlaverock were matched in formality a century earlier by the circular plan of the now-destroyed royal site of Queenborough.

The tradition of ceremony is continued in these castles from the 12th century. The contrast between wide doors and stairs, for two people side by side, and the narrower private stair gives us clues as to the routes of ceremony. There are now even more points along the way, entrances to the courtyards, to the hall, to the lord's lodgings block and to the great chamber, where the guest might be greeted or held. There are lobbies at the entrance to the great chamber at Goodrich (considerately with access to a latrine), between the hall and the chambers at Wardour and a guard room at the entrance to Bolton castle hall. The best example of the planning providing a ceremonial route of access to the lord and control of visitors is perhaps at Warkworth. The access from the outer court to the inner and the tower, is obscure; either a passage past the kitchen or through the chapel which separates the two courts. Neither

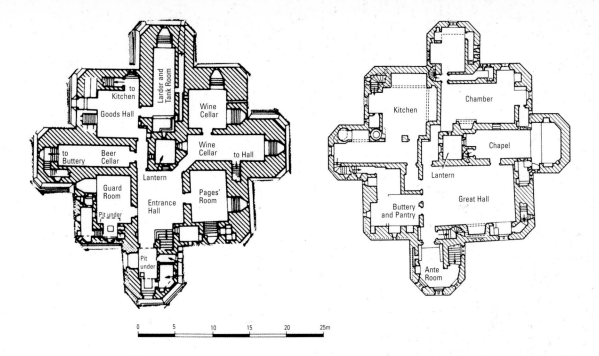

Larder and Tank Room

to
Kitchen

Goods Hall

Wine
Cellar

to
Buttery

Beer
Cellar

Wine
Cellar

to Hall

Guard
Room

Lantern

Pages'
Room

Pit under

Entrance
Hall

Pit
under

Kitchen

Chamber

Chapel

Lantern

Great Hall

Buttery
and Pantry

Ante
Room

0   5   10   15   20   25m

48 *(above)* **Plan of the great tower of Warkworth castle.**

would be obvious to a visitor coming in the great gate. The actual entrance in the tower leads to a dark hallway with a bewildering number of doors opening off it, most of them into stores. The stair leads up to a lobby before the great chamber, or private hall, of the Percy earl. Unless you were a regular visitor, it would have been difficult, if not impossible, to find your way without the guidance of a page or minder.

The rows of uniform lodgings built to house the lesser members of these late medieval households are sometimes to be seen in the fireplaces set along the curtain wall, but are preserved well at Dartington Hall. Each was a bed-sitting room with a fireplace and a door to a latrine; the plan is repeated on the ground and first floors. They are very similar to the rooms provided for the Fellows of an Oxford college, or the priests of a private chantry; both would also have their common hall and chapel. This tells us both of the social standing of the men these lodgings were meant to house, but

49 *(right)* **The hall windows as seen from the outside of Bolton castle.**

50 *(above)* Reconstructed view of the enclosure of Stokesay castle.

51 *(below)* The interior of the hall at Stokesay castle. The building dates to the 13th century (shortly before Lawrence de Ludlow added his chamber tower), but the roof was completely redesigned in the 15th century to remove the aisles, while the stairs (at the low end of the hall) lead to chambers in an earlier tower. This is an example of the role of the hall at the centre of castle life continuing throughout the period, as well as an example of a small castle at the boundary with a manor house.

also speaks of the two communities, brought together in the service of their lord.

THE 15TH CENTURY AND LATER

During the third quarter of the 15th century Sir William Herbert built Raglan castle, which epitomizes, if any single building can, the castles of the later Middle Ages (**53** and see **89**). It had the advantage of being built on what was effectively a new site. The plan is not symmetrical but is carefully organized around two courtyards and a great tower. The outer court, with the great gate, kitchen and services, is separated from the inner one by the great hall and chapel, which are therefore accessible from both areas. The inner court has ranges of lodgings around it, mainly individual rooms. The upper end of the great hall gives access to the state apartments at first-floor level. They pivot around a presence chamber, marked out on the exterior by the heraldic carvings around its magnificent windows. On either side of it stretch the main suites for the household officers, such as the one in the first floor of the gatehouse. From it a bridge leads to the great hexagonal tower reserved for the lord's apartments, with its own kitchen, outer and inner chambers. The tower sits astride the approach to the gatehouse. On the one hand, these two sheltered the wide presence chamber windows from attack, but on the other the siting ensured that the full power and display of the Herbert lords was immediately impressed on any visitor. Castles in England are often deemed to end with Thornbury built between 1511 and 1522; it was the last building with something like a serious attempt at defence while still remaining a great magnate's residence. There are two points to be made: one that this is a position that only holds for Wales and England south of the Pennines. It also only applies to the castle as a military institution. As a civil building, the castle survived long afterwards, into the 17th century. The domestic accommodation of an important Elizabethan or Jacobean house revolved around the great chamber, increasingly replacing the great hall as the scene even for major entertainments such as masques. The idea of the self-contained suite of rooms for an individual member of the household, however, continues right to the end of the 17th century. Only when the domestic rooms in the great houses are welded into a single unit, can the castle household, a set of officers with separate status and lives, arranged around a great magnate, be said to have ended.

In continental Europe, the castle merged much more easily with the great house – the survival of the word château in French is an example, and castles continued in use in northern England, Scotland and Ireland longer than in southern England. This is connected in part with the widespread building of a particular type of castle, the so-called tower house. Its roots and popularity tell us about the societies concerned, and about the role of castles in general. We have seen, at Stokesay (**50**), Hopton or Longthorpe how some lesser lords, around the year 1300, built detached chamber towers in their small castles or manor houses: the same can be seen in the north of England at Edlingham (see **7**). In later 14th-century Scotland we can see two important men doing the same. The Duke of Albany rebuilt Doune castle, with a high residential tower for himself attached to his great hall. At Threave the Earl of Douglas built a wholly detached tower for his use, with a ground-floor hall (recently exposed by excavation); when the castle was put into a new state of defence in the 1440s the hall was left outside the new wall.

It is the widespread adoption of the tower house that is most informative, because they answered two needs for the men who built them. The tower houses are essentially the chamber towers, which developed in the later 13th century; a ground floor (usually vaulted against fire) for storage and a hall or great chamber on the first floor with a private chamber above are the minimum essentials (**52, 54**). They provide the sort of domestic accommodation a lord required for himself. What they did not provide was the additional rooms and buildings for his large household, which the great magnates needed. Secondly, a tower could be made defensible, not against a siege, but against a raid by neighbours or a riot; as such they are common wherever such things were likely, as with the Marches of English land in France. The towers were built, above all, by the lesser lords of Ireland and Scotland, many of whom had advanced from being tenants of the knightly class to being freeholders of their estates. In Ireland the proliferation of these towers in some regions followed the establishing of many new lordships as a new pattern of settlement was established. This is the more marked by the way that tower houses proved often to be

52 *(below)* Reconstruction of a tower house in Ireland. The rooms are adequate for only a small household.

53 (above) View of Raglan castle. The design has three main elements; the outer ward with the main gate, the inner ward providing retainer's lodgings, and the great tower for the lord's lodgings.

54 (below) Audley's castle, Co. Down; a small tower house.

the first form in which Irish Gaelic lords (and some Scots in the West Highlands as well) built castles. Significantly this happened at a period between 1350 and 1450 when the Gaelic lords were becoming more concerned with tightening their control over land rather than simply over their followers.

In neither Scotland nor Ireland were the towers the only form of castle in the 15th or 16th centuries. In Scotland, as well as the tower at Threave, the Douglas Earls maintained Bothwell and Tantallon. In Ireland the Butler Earls of Ormonde were centred at Kilkenny castle, while their relatives built the enclosure castle at Grannagh; the Earls of Desmond built and extended the two large castles of Newcastle and Askeaton. These make the point that towers were for the men who had smaller households to maintain, as well as fewer men to defend a large perimeter. In this way the late medieval towers in these areas remind us of the basic functions of castles: to establish control of an estate, to accommodate the household needed to maintain that control and to provide the physical strength required to prevent the lord from being ejected through the sort of force likely to be deployed against him. Before we concern ourselves with the defence, we should look at the provision for the extended households made in the larger castles (some would say the true castles). This means the service side, and the links through them, to the supporting region around.

4 THE OUTER CORE

If we continue with the metaphor of the first chapter, around the inner core of the lord's working and personal household there existed further layers, like an onion. These comprised the people who supported the castle and its inner core, themselves working and living both inside and outside the castle. The lord of the castle directly employed some while the lives of others were dominated by the existence of the castle. All of them came together in the great hall. They met for the courts held there and for the feasts; for some an invitation to participate, but for the servants these meant work, at least before being able to enjoy the leftovers. The main work was the preparing and serving of food, which was a matter taken very seriously throughout the Middle Ages, emphasized, perhaps, by the continual presence of the people outside who did not have access either to the society or, indeed, to food at all.

THE GREAT HALL

The serving of food on great occasions was the most complicated of the activities carried on in the great hall. One of the roots of medieval lordship was the world of the Germanic or Celtic chieftain feasting with his war band of henchmen, and formal meals in the company of his supporters were one of the essential elements of a lord's life. His position was physically expressed by being seated

55 *(right)* A reconstruction of the interior of the great hall at Kenilworth castle in the 1390s.

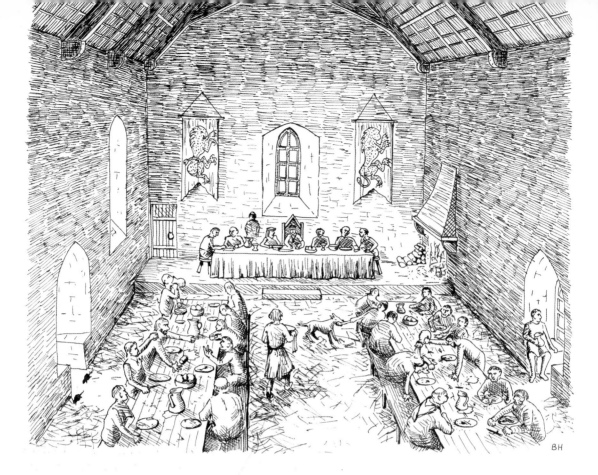

56 *(above)* A reconstruction of dinner in the great hall of a 13th-century castle (Greencastle, Co. Down), showing the high table at one end and the other tables down the body of the hall; it omits the servants however.

at the centre of the high table placed across one end of the hall; he looked down the whole hall and was visible from everywhere in it (**55, 56**). His closest friends or associates joined him at this table, their position equally visible. Lesser men sat at tables stretching the length of the main body of the hall. These tables were simply boards set on movable trestles, so they could be put away after the meal, to clear the space for entertainment or business.

> The king's brother, the Count of Artois, stood facing his majesty ready to serve his meat, while beside the count the good Count Jean de Soissons wielded a carving knife. Imbert de Beaujeu, later High Constable of France, with Enguerrand de Coucy and Archimbault de Bourbon, were on guard at the king's table, and behind them stood some thirty of their knights, in tunics of silk, to keep guard over their lords. Behind these knights stood a great company of sergeants, in suits of taffeta embroidered with the arms of the Count of Poitiers ... It was said that no less than three thousand knights were present at that occasion.

This description of a great court feast of Louis IX of France in 1244 emphasizes several things. Without believing the figure of 3000, there were many people there; serving them with food can have been no easy task. Great men were served by men of the rank below, and so on, so that the total present was steadily inflated. This was a major royal occasion; ordinary lords on ordinary days lived in much lesser state, but this was in the middle of the 13th century. By the 15th century ceremony had greatly increased and filtered down the ranks of the aristocracy. The account also lists and stresses the elaborate and costly dress of the chief men, as well as their supporters; these were colourful occasions.

Both the way food was served and the ceremony with which it happened meant that there was a lot of preparation required. For the high table the food would be brought up on dishes. It was elaborately decorated and presented, and was then carved at the table before the lord (57). The people sitting at the other tables in the body of the hall ate from dishes shared between more than one – two if you were lucky but usually four. The dishes were called messes; those who shared a dish were messmates. Here the food was already carved and was eaten by picking out pieces with hands and putting them on a trencher of stale bread, which acted as a plate. The same distinction applied to drink: the lord and those on the high table might have individual cups, but the rest drank from a common jug. Both the main dishes for the high table and filling up the messes needed space and time, as did cutting the trenchers. Filling the jugs with beer or wine was the same, so that it was essential to have rooms not just for cooking but also for dishing up the food and drink. This was made more necessary by the general reluctance of medieval lords to have their kitchens beside their halls. On the one hand, they were probably not keen to have the noise, smell and crowds attendant on a kitchen mixed up with their social events, but, more importantly, the kitchen was a serious fire risk best kept safely isolated.

As we have seen, the whole Middle Ages saw a steady rise in the emphasis and elaboration of the lord's accommodation, and in particular the great, or presence, chamber. At times people have been led to argue that the increasing use of the great chamber for meals meant that the great hall was devalued. This is certainly untrue for the 13th and 14th centuries, to judge by the physical evidence of the money spent on them. We have seen how John of Gaunt made the great hall the centrepiece of his design for the rebuilding of Kenilworth castle at the end of the 14th century (see **44** and **62**). It was decorated with the most elaborate traceried windows and stone panelling, which can still be seen; its width demanded an elaborate roof structure (see **55**), now lost. John's half-nephew, John Holand

57 *(above)* The lord is served at high table, from the Luttrell Psalter.

rebuilt Dartington Hall at the same period. Drawings made in 1805 show that its hall was roofed with a revolutionary new design, the hammer beam. This seems to have been a prototype of the magnificent roof erected for Richard II over the great hall of Westminster palace in the 1390s. As well as its visual appeal, where the tiers of beams emphasize the height of the roof, it was a practical design, for it allowed much greater spans to be covered without internal supports; the aisles of the traditional wide halls could be removed and the whole space thrown open. The Tudor revolutions in land holding saw the building of many houses; in all of them, the great hall was a prominent feature. These halls might not see their lord as often as those of the 12th century, but they were vital to his castle or house none the less.

THE SERVICE ROOMS

The separation of the chambers from the hall had an effect on the service end of the buildings as well. During the last years of the 12th century two service rooms and a detached kitchen were added at the west end of the great hall at Clarendon Palace. The Bishop's palace at Lincoln has the same arrangements from the early 13th century, with doors to the two service rooms opening off the great hall and a central door between them leading down a passage to the kitchen (see **34**). The arrangement at Clarendon or Lincoln proved to be very long lasting, surviving into the 16th century at least. The triple

58 *(right)* One of the hearths and ovens in the kitchen at Kenilworth castle.

doors in particular seem to have been thought of as essential for the service end of a hall. It was convenient as the two side rooms reflected the basic division of the household servants into those dealing with food – the pantry – and those concerned with drink – the buttery – while the central passage allowed for the sort of formal entry of food for the lord that medieval ceremony demanded.

The three doors were even built when it appears to have been awkward, to the point of not in fact reflecting the existence of two rooms and a passage behind. At Goodrich castle the south end of the hall has three doors, but one leads down to a cellar below the tower attached, while at the hall level there is no sign of a division in the tower corresponding to the other two doors (see **42**). In fact the kitchen lies to the south-east and there can never have been a passage south from the hall to it. By around 1300, when Goodrich was built, it would appear that the three-door arrangement was ingrained into castle planning. A further advantage of the scheme was apparent from the time of Lincoln palace at least. The two service rooms did not need to be high, yet they were attached to the end of the great hall, whose gable was raised as high as any other building in the castle. There was an obvious opportunity here to put a chamber over the service rooms, reached either directly from the hall or else from the main entrance porch to it. With the increasing emphasis on the orientation of the hall in the 14th century, which we saw in the last chapter, this chamber situated over the service end of the hall could not be assigned to the lord or to his immediate household. It was, however, perfectly placed to accommodate a senior household official, such as the butler, chamberlain or the chief purchasing clerk, who was at the one time senior enough to warrant a fine chamber, but who was particularly associated with the supervision of the services of the castle.

The Lincoln kitchen is a four-sided building (it would be square if the lie of the land permitted) with a great hearth in each of the corners, making it easy to build the hood and flue over the fireplace. Nothing evokes the scale of the medieval dinners better than the size of the castle kitchens, and their hearths, whether they are in a freestanding kitchen as at Lincoln; in one sited in a corner tower, as at Bodiam or Raglan; or set against the curtain wall as at Kenilworth (**58** and see **44**). Every time they evoke the casual royal command of King John who ordered new kitchens at Marlborough and Ludgershall castles: 'in each kitchen shall be made a hearth for the cooking of two or three oxen'. It was usual to build into the side of each hearth a circular domed oven, in which was placed lighted fuel; this heated the walls enough so that, when the fire was removed, the ovens were sufficiently hot to bake bread or pies. A second important room beside the kitchen, also with a hearth or oven, was the brew house. Beer was essential to a medieval household; apart from anything else, brewing sterilized the water. Documentary evidence refers to other rooms or buildings connected to the castle kitchen, such as a scullery, or slaughterhouse, larders, etc.; the kitchen was not just a single room but the centre of a complex.

THE FOOD

There are two main sources for what was cooked in the kitchen, medieval recipe collections and accounts of feasts, and the results of excavations conducted beside them to recover the waste products of the cooking (**59, 60**). The recipes are a subject all of their own, the food heavily spiced and served with complicated sauces; if the ingredients were as pure and strong tasting as modern ones, then the food was powerful stuff.

Excavations have provided some information, but as always there are caveats. The results of excavation are never straightforward to explain. The main body of evidence is of bones thrown out at the time and then dug up by archaeologists. The first uncertainty is that we cannot know how the bones reached the position in which we find them. This is best expressed as the problem of explaining how a single bone of a weasel might be recovered from the drain of the kitchen at Barnard castle in a collection of bones described as being the remains of a feast. Did a person bring the animal to the castle, or did it come in pursuit of mice? If the animal died in the drain, was this bone the most robust survivor of the whole skeleton, the rest of which rotted (or was washed) away, or was not recovered by

59 *(above and below)* Reconstruction of a medieval castle kitchen and a group of medieval jugs and cooking pots.

the excavators? Is this a single bone from a carcass that died elsewhere so that just the one bone was carried in by a dog, or kicked around by a kitchen boy? A second problem is that we do not know why the animals were in the castle. If they were for food, were they there to be eaten only at the high table, or by everyone? Some animals were not for food but were still there in the service of man; dogs for hunting or as pets, cats for catching mice, horses for riding or pulling carts. Some were there in spite of man, such as the rats and mice in the stores and drains, or the jackdaws in the chimneys and sparrows in the stable yard. Obviously some animals may have been there for more than one purpose.

The excavations at Portchester castle illustrate one of the more useful approaches to the evidence of bones. It was noticed here that the patterns of bones from the inner and outer areas of the castle were different. In the inner ward, where the hall and lodgings lay, the bones were overwhelmingly of animals and birds used for food. Further, the bones of the animals represented in the inner ward did not include those from the parts of the body that are not edible, such as the skull, and there were very few horse bones; both were found in the outer ward. Butchery and the keeping of animals (other than pets) took place away from the inner core of the castle life. Portchester was interesting also because it was a castle set inside

60 *(above)* Cooking food, from the Luttrell Psalter.

a Roman and Anglo-Saxon fort (see **5**), and the pattern of the bones from the different periods could be compared. One of the differences was that the bones from the castle levels were more often chopped up; they were used to make stock and stews, as the elaborate cookery of a castle succeeded the life of a fort. The animals, both at Portchester and at other sites, tended to be from animals killed at an age when they had reached maturity but little more. These were animals bred specifically for food, rather than being eaten at the end of a life of either giving milk or wool, or of pulling ploughs or carts; the products of a more specialized agricultural organization.

Two comments need to be made about the number of species present, which invariably differs from castle to castle. The first is that there are some sites where the number of deer bones are much greater: 20 or 30 per cent of the bones at Sandal and Okehampton castles were of deer. Urban castles unsurprisingly show much lower figures, but so do some castles which we would think to be rural and involved in hunting, less than 5 per cent at Portchester, and the same at Hadleigh castle. Again, the individual assemblage is less informative than comparing a group of sites and seeking a norm. The local resources are not the only source of food, however. Where fish bones have been recovered in excavations, all castles produce evidence of sea fish, although an inland site such as Barnard or Sandal has fewer species than a coastal one such as Portchester. Fish was required for Lent and on Fridays so it had to be supplied either by local fishermen or through the market.

61 *(above)* Reconstructed aerial view of Barnard castle, showing the extent of the outer courts.

All this food needed to be stored somewhere. Traditionally one of the ways that we have explained any room, especially one on the ground floor, which lacked fireplace, latrine, good windows or any of the recognized signs of occupancy, as being a store room. Undoubtedly some, if not most, were, but they may also have been used for servants sleeping as well. In some cases we can see a hierarchy of these store rooms. Below the large hall at Chepstow is a fine vaulted cellar; it is reached down stairs from the service passage, where there are cupboards for valuables, and outside it is a platform up to which goods could be lifted from a boat in the River Wye below. Most of the store rooms in the tower at Warkworth open from the entrance lobby, but one is accessed only by stairs from the hall above. Both of these seem to be places where the supplies of spices or wine was kept, more expensive items which needed to to be kept safely.

THE OUTER COURT

Animals and cooking take us beyond the immediate environs of the kitchen and into the outer court generally. This is an area of which we know much less than the basic core of the castle (**61**). It often lay outside the main wall of the castle itself, comprising buildings and functions which were not central to the lord's life and which he deemed expendable. The buildings themselves might be less substantial than those of the inner court, and so more prone to destruction. They were also prone to being sold off in later periods, but in some cases, as with Barnard castle, they are still visible as empty spaces, although they were once occupied, probably by timber buildings now vanished. The principal requirement for the life of any castle would have been one, or more, stables. The foundations of one have been excavated at Farleigh Hungerford, and the remains of a second uncovered at Goodrich; both within outer wards. At Goodrich it was built with a central passage between two rows of stalls; the horses apparently entered from one end. The walls at Farleigh Hungerford were substantial and buttressed, implying an upper floor, presumably to store hay, and perhaps for the grooms to live in. Horses were essential to the life of a castle. A lord with any pretensions to an active political life needed at least one war horse (see **2**); he also needed horses for hunting and for riding from place to place. His journeys involved moving large amounts of servants and baggage; this needed more horses, if of lower quality. The value of horses and the care they required meant that stables were essential.

As well as stables, there must have been other buildings in or beside every castle. The baggage and stores of a castle needed carts and therefore sheds for them. Hunting meant hounds and therefore kennels, while hawking needed mews. The animals had to be looked after by grooms and huntsmen; the carts meant carters. Both men and animals needed food and stores of all sorts. It is unlikely that they could have contained all the requirements of a castle, however, especially such things as the hay or unground corn. Surveys of castles often mention granaries or barns, mills as well as craft shops, such as smithies. Few, if any, survive above ground but they must have been there, with the staff they needed to serve them.

PARKS AND GARDENS

The immediate surroundings of the castle contained areas devoted to entertainment. The latter meant hunting and hawking, the main recreations of the nobility in the Middle Ages. Both involved the conservation of game, for the landscape as a whole had been too heavily farmed since the 11th century for there to be enough natural habitats preserved to satisfy the demands of the hunt which was overwhelmingly aimed at deer. While hawks should be flown in wooded and hedged country, and falcons work best in open land, deer hunting by the 11th century needed areas of country set aside for it. The royal forests were the most prominent of such areas, but most lords had a park for hunting. Their boundaries may still be found either on maps or in the countryside, marked by the substantial ditches built to prevent the deer escaping. They are inevitably wide in their extent and often survived long after the castle had been replaced by a country house; hunting in the medieval style lasted well into the 18th century, especially on the Continent.

Connected to the deer park, often physically so, was the garden. By the 14th century most castles had a garden, at least if the lord lived it in frequently. These were pure pleasure gardens, consisting of lawns and flowerbeds; the lawns were usually not just of mown grass but also of longer grass sown with native wild flowers. Many of the flowerbeds were raised beside paths and their common features were raised benches of sods and trellises of climbing plants, either straight or enclosing seats. The formality of their design, as we see it in the manuscript pictures, contrasted with the open parkland that in many cases lay beyond. Besides these gardens there were orchards and herb gardens, which helped to supply the castle with food as well as being attractive in their own right. A further feature would be a tiltyard for jousting; a possible survival to the present day being the one at Dartington Hall.

These were all physical features that formed part of the immediate surrounds of many castles. The evidence is mainly either in the form of contemporary surveys and descriptions of castles, or else from paintings. Occasionally they reach accounts, as with the three pence paid in 1284 for watering the lawn at Conway, and the 16 shillings paid for turves there. Although they were all physical features that should have left at least some traces in the ground, we can point to few remains of buildings and none of the less substantial aspects. It is not easy to detect the remains of garden paths and flowerbeds, but when it can be done (conceivably linked to pollen analysis of soil buried beneath turf banks), it is a fascinating exercise. What we can see are the remains of small enclosures, which fit the description of what a garden should look like, but whether these are

62 *(above)* Aerial view of the inner court at Kenilworth castle. The hall with a tower at either end lies at the top of the picture; the lord's chambers run off to its left, the service rooms and kitchen to its right. The 16th-century garden lies to the right of the service range and older great tower.

gardens, cabbage patches or yards is almost impossible to decide.

The castle of Tintagel is a romantic conceit, founded for its Arthurian associations rather than for any practical reason. The headland on which it is built is windswept and small enclosures have been identified as gardens. Unlike parks they have no distinctive boundaries or wide areas, nor do they last long untouched by fashion and re-planning. It is likely that the remains we see of later gardens were the sites of the medieval ones. Beside the lord's great tower of the 15th century at Ashby-de-la-Zouche is a 16th- or 17th-century garden terrace (**63**); beside the old great tower of Kenilworth castle is a 16th-century formal garden (**62**), both are very possibly on the site of the medieval ones. The entrance to Kenilworth is through an earthwork and across a broad dam, which has been known since at least the 17th century as the 'tiltyard', and may well have been used for the later medieval jousts (see **44**); there is another at Dartington Hall.

Along with gardens and parks, part entertainment and part resource are the fish ponds. These survive better on the ground, because their remains are conspicuous and because they are

obviously sited with access to water. The ponds were clearly for fish production but they overlapped with the idea of the ornamental pool and the castle moat. Linked to them was often the castle water mill, also using a water supply brought along a leat.

The land around Bodiam castle, the formal castle built by Sir Edward Dalyngrigge in the later 14th century, has recently been meticulously surveyed and its interpretation has become something of a type site, much quoted. This has proposed an approach route to the castle, from the south end of the village west of the castle, from which he could see it in the distance. He then lost sight of it as he went along between the dams and artificial ponds, linked to the castle moat, only to come upon it from the south, rising directly up from the moat. The path took him past the south and east sides, where the larger windows proclaimed the position of the great hall and Sir Edward's lodgings, round the north of the castle to the great gatehouse. There are two problems in accepting this suggested approach, however. The first is that it is only an unproven suggestion and it is a very complex route. The second is that as it enters the castle precinct it comes very close to, or may even traverse land belonging to Robertsbridge abbey, and it then proceeds through the mill yard and the service area of the castle. It may be that medieval people were less snobbish about this, but it seems odd. It is more likely that the entry was organized to run from the north end of the village, past the castle fish ponds, to come out opposite the show front of the castle. This is simpler, avoids any problems with ownership and still brings a visitor to the show front.

THE CASTLE AND THE LAND

One of the reasons for looking for these features is that they link the castle to the countryside around it. This link is inherent in all that has been discussed so far; the lords of castles were the holders of great landed estates, some of which they did not lease out but farmed themselves. Very often these lands were those which lay closest to the castle, so that it took on the role of the main centre of a large farm, with all that this implies in terms of buildings, equipment and people. The farms of the Middle Ages needed many people to run them; like the factories of recent society they were the principal source of employment, and their organization dictated where many of the people lived. This brings us to the question of the role played by castles in the pattern of human settlement.

European agriculture of the period between the end of the 9th century and the beginning of the 12th saw a massive reorganization. It became based on two expensive machines, the great plough, typically pulled by eight oxen, and the water mill. Both needed investment, large fields and large-scale production of corn if they were to be used efficiently; if they were, the mouths of a rising population ensured that they would be profitable. The need for capital beyond the resources of any one free farmer pushed him to join others in a co-operative system of farming. At the same time, in the aftermath of the invasions during the 9th and 10th centuries by the Vikings and others, the lords who had successfully beaten off these attacks wished to tighten their grip on their estates and their control over tenants. The result was that the small villages, hamlets and isolated farms of the earlier age were abandoned in favour of larger villages tied to the estates of the new aristocracy. These villages formed the basis of the reorganization of the Church into parishes, the responsibility of a single priest, with precisely defined, immutable boundaries; the modern pattern of European rural settlement was created. The result of a massive reordering of settlements may perhaps be seen in the regular plans of many of the villages of North Yorkshire and Durham, the legacy of the harrying of the north by King William in 1168–9. The lords imposed regularity on the settlements, quite possibly at the same time as they created them from an earlier pattern. This was the role of lordship, but it was not necessarily accompanied by the building of castles.

The main sign that we can use to study this is the parish church. It was difficult to move both for institutional reasons (the Church discouraged any change to consecrated land) or cultural ones (the graveyard contained the community's ancestors). The church is therefore often the main fixed point in the landscape. Inevitably, perhaps, it seems often to have been linked with the new lordships and estates which accompanied the reorganization of agriculture. Even if it was peasant initiative that lay behind the move to consolidated settlements, the church is likely to have been sited at the focus of them. The relationship between castles and churches is often a clue as to the place of the castle in the settlement pattern of the immediate area.

On some occasions, castle and church are close, even to the extent of the parish church being set within an outer enclosure of the castle (see **63**). It is usually almost impossible to establish firmly which came first. Undoubtedly in some cases, through either documentary evidence or the dating of architectural features in the church, we are fairly sure that the church is the earlier. At Sulgrave or Goltho, the castle can be shown to have taken over an earlier enclosure set beside the church. This may be the usual explanation of those places where the two are close; the castle is the successor of an earlier estate centre. Where the church is then enclosed within part of the castle, we may interpret it in two ways. We may see this as an act of conquest, appropriating the village church into the lord's domain, as he took over the community too. Alternatively, we may stress the continuing links between church and community, and see the association of the castle with the church as an association with the community. The two may not be as exclusive as they sound; one attitude may even give way to the other. In either case, the castle is likely to come after the settlement, rather than the village following the castle.

Although we may suspect that the castle is an intrusion into the village and its community, it may have resulted in the reorganization

64 *(above)* Aerial view of Framlingham castle and village form the south showing the line of approach from the village to the castle gate.

of its fabric. Many villages appear to have been planned to focus in some way on the castle, either positively in the sense of leading up to it, or else negatively in that they are separated from it. In this planning the church may also be involved, being set at the other end of the village, for example, from the castle. In such a case, it is very difficult to test whether we are looking at an instance of reorganization and re-planning, or one of new settlement and a new village.

At Framlingham castle, its location certainly seems to be peripheral to the village centred east of the parish church; when a market was established, it too focused on the church rather than the castle (**64**). We may suspect reorganization in a number of cases. The present fabric of the castle of Ashby-de-la Zouche is mostly of the late Middle Ages, but the site is old; the association with the parish church – and the separation from the rest of the village is clear. A new castle was built at Bolingbroke in the early 13th century in the plain to the south of the 12th-century site; the present church and village appear to have been at least re-oriented. The church faces the gate of the new castle with the village stretching to east and west along a street to the north of the church which thus, like Ashby, seems to separate (or link) the castle and its community. The 14th-century castle of Bolton was the culmination of the Scrope family building up their lands in this part of Yorkshire, and the village must have been re-planned to reflect the new castle in the fourteenth century (**67**). Against this are the rare examples of Edlingham (see **7**) and Maxstoke, where the 14th-century castles were built away from the church and village.

The story in England contrasts with that of Ireland. Here the reform of the Church whereby the parish was introduced came later, and into a landscape with fewer (if any) villages settlements. The parishes were set up only in the later 12th century, at the time of the English seizure and partition of the land. The new parishes in the areas of the English lordships were often structured around the lesser estates and manors and the association of church and castle is often close. In this case, however, often no nucleated settlement has survived, if one ever existed. Again, the tower houses in parts of Ireland, which were seized by new families in the 14th century, seem to have formed the basis of a new pattern of settlement. They were not the centres of new villages, for the landscape saw the scattering of the earlier nucleated settlement in favour of dispersed houses,

linked to an agricultural economy increasingly dependent on cattle farming. The contrast both points up the association of the village idea with a different agriculture, but also the way that it was probably more usual for the castle to follow, and then possibly modify English settlement, rather than create it anew.

CASTLES AND TOWNS

Castles had a much greater impact on the development of towns than of villages. The large household of a castle needed supplies in a quantity and of a variety beyond the capacity of a village to produce; it needed a market. Towns in the 11th century were usually the centres of royal administration and this probably explains why the castles of William I were often sited there; to seize the country he needed to dominate the centres of power. The castles placed within an existing town were normally built at the edge of it, either for security, restricting the front it exposed to the towns-people, or to limit the amount of damage done to the fabric of the town, although the figures given in the Domesday Survey of the numbers of houses destroyed would argue against this.

Beside this, in the 12th century lords discovered that a borough, with its steady rents coming in without any effort on their part, was a good investment. The foundation of a castle frequently, therefore, led to the foundation of a borough to serve it (**65**). The combination of town and castle is best seen in the western areas of Britain where the new lordships of the Anglo-Normans aimed to introduce a whole new economy into the region. Cardiff owes its existence today to the reuse of the Roman fort by Robert fitz Hamon or William I for his castle; Carrickfergus is another example of town, port and castle (**66**). Edward I founded towns beside most of his north Wales castles as part of the process of conquest, establishing a nucleus of a loyal population as well as bringing the locality into an economic network dominated by the English. In Ulster, the castle, port, market place and town of Carrickfergus were founded together to act as the chief place of the new Earldom of the English after 1177. A town that is dependent on a castle alone for its livelihood is vulnerable to the demise of the castle.

CASTLES AND THE PLANNED LANDSCAPE

Given that the main role of a castle was to dominate the society and land around it, it is not surprising that we may detect the signs that the whole surrounding area was planned in relation to the castle and to reinforce the message of the dominance. This is clearly seen in the urban settlements, particularly those where the town was either founded with the castle or followed it. Warkworth castle lies at the head of the borough street and blocks the approach to it at the head of the neck of the peninsula on which it lies (see **35**). The great Percy lion on the Earl's tower faces down the main street, in case anyone should forget just whose town this was. The market place of Richmond was laid out in front of the castle with a new church, while the old parish church lies a little way beyond in a tangle of small streets (**68**). It looks as though when the castle was founded a borough (and new church to serve it) was also laid out beside the older core. Farnham castle stands at the head of the Market Place of the borough with the parish church at the other end. The two units, castle and town may be bound together: the 12th-century earthworks of Pleshey castle are joined to the ditch of the borough founded with it. The two may appear in rivalry; the great tower of Rochester castle appears to confront the cathedral, just as the west tower of Lincoln cathedral (itself possibly the Bishop's first castle) confronts the royal castle. The castle's presence was not always dominant as time wore on. It is just possible to make out the lines of streets of the new town founded by William de Albini in the middle of the 12th century outside his castle of New Buckenham, but the settlement now is reduced to the size of a small village. The demise of the castle must

66 *(above)* Carrickfergus castle from the south; a visiting mechant ship's view. The port and the town were established with the castle as the centre of the new Lordship of Ulster, created after 1170.

67 *(above)* The castle of Bolton seen from the village; the village street (on the right) is aligned to lead straight to the castle entrance.

have contributed to the desertion of the town. In Cumbria the castle of Brough led to the foundation of a little borough town, marked by its wide street leading away from the castle gate. In time the commercial attractions of the main road a little way off outstripped those of the castle and resulted in a second town, Market Brough, being established and then regularized by the lords.

The story is similar with the village settlements. There are examples where the village has been clearly arranged to lead up to the castle: Bolton castle gate faces down the village green (**67**). The Neville family also built a new castle at Sherriff Hutton as well as at Bolton and added a new section to the village with a green along with it. In Buckinghamshire the village of Boarhunt was aligned with the castle; it is now deserted but the subject of a remarkable 15th century plan or view showing it. By contrast, the prosperity of the De Caux family resulted in re-planning part of the village of Laxton in Northamptonshire, but on different lines; here the castle and village were firmly separated by a bank. The castle site was also planned to give access to, and control of, its resources so castles are often sited at the junction of two or more of these. The most common is to put it where the better arable land gives way to pasture or rougher ground, which forms the basis for the park. Likewise a riverine situation will help with fishponds, mills or moats.

What is interesting is to see how all these different elements, unsurprising in themselves, were put together. This resulted in two things. Firstly we can see that the castle siting and the management of the landscape were part of the same large-scale planning process. In a passive way, the siting of the castles of Odo of Bayeux or others, which we saw earlier, reflect the distribution of their lands. The proliferation of motte castles in areas of disturbance and raids is also a response to the landscape. On the other hand, in the widest sense the founding of castles was an active part of the whole process of the expansion and organization of farm production in the 11th and 12th centuries. The union of castle parish and village is clearly this on a local scale. On a wider scale, in the north-east of Normandy, the lesser castles of the great lords are set on the marginal lands away from the older centres, to bring these under the overall control of the great lords. In Norfolk, in the late 11th century, the castles are sited less by the old arable lands and more on the margins. These last were the areas of opportunity with fewer vested interests to the

68 *(right)* Aerial view of Richmond castle and town.

building up of a wide lordship. It was in the same spirit that the castles of the Celtic lands were founded by their English or Anglicized lords, to bring a new management to the land and its resources, through more intensive farming and trade.

The second aspect of this was the siting of castles to be dominant features of the landscape. One way to do this, of course, was to place the castle on a prominent hill top, as in the Alps or on the cliffs above the Rhine. This had its disadvantages: you could see a long way over the surrounding lands, but it was a long way to go to do something about it, and a long weary way up the hill back again. It was also all too easy for people to ignore the lord perched high up on a hill away from the roads or action. It was better to focus the land and its routes and views on the castle instead. In the 11th-century Castle Acre was set across the Peddar's Way where it crossed the River Nar (see **7**). Coming from the south, the road was diverted to take it through the town, but the view along the approach was the same. The castle stood on the rise beyond the river, with the Abbey to the west and the town between. From the north, the road ran through the Castle Park, with the castle silhouetted at the edge of the drop into the river valley. In either case, the castle was the focus of the view across the whole landscape. Barnard castle lies on a cliff at the point where the main road out of the town crosses the River Tees (**69**). The castle is the first thing a visitor to the town would have seen; in the past this would have been seen in military terms, as 'controlling the crossing' but it is just as much visually dominant. In the 14th century the rising family of the Beauchamp Earls of Warwick rebuilt the east and south fronts of their castle in Warwick. The castle was sited at the south edge of the town on a cliff over the river Avon; below the castle was the mill. Originally it may be that the castle was approached through the town from the north. When they rebuilt the east front, the Earls gave the castle a magnificent new gatehouse and two remarkable

corner towers: one is ten-sided, the other trefoil-shaped in plan. The road from London approached the town and castle from the south. Anyone coming along this travelled first through the castle park for about a mile, and saw, from the top of Gallows Hill, the castle and town before them on the cliff over the river. The façade was dominated by the hall in the south range and the trefoil-shaped Caesar's tower, with its double tier of machicolations at the angle. A new bridge led over the river to a steep climb up a semi-circular road to the great gate.

These are cases where the castle is sited to impress everyone approaching it. The effect could be more restricted, aimed at guests already admitted to the precinct. Across the defensive lake at Kenilworth lies an enclosure, reached only by water; known as the 'Pleasance', it was built in 1414 as a place for picnics. From it, the guest has a view across the lake to the main range of the castle, the hall and John of Gaunt's lodgings. Whatever the route in to Bodiam, there is another visual effect in the grounds. To the north, on the hill above the moat and looking down on the castle is an earthen platform. This is now known as the Gun platform but it seems both to be older, and likely to be made deliberately as a place from which to admire the castle in its moats below. In both cases we may have places designed for a walk or row as a recreation, with a view of the castle contrived as well. The same can be seen in reverse: castles could be made to be looked at with awe but they could also provide views of the land around purely for its own sake. In the great tower of Carrickfergus castle a small stair rises from the third floor to the battlements and roof above. This is not for defence, for the third floor was the lord's chamber, and he would not appreciate soldiers passing through it regularly; there was the main stair rising from the ground floor for them. This is a pattern which occurs occasionally at all periods afterwards, a stair which rises to the roof from the lord's rooms. It must be for the use of him and his guests, to go up to the roof to look at the view, perhaps as an after-dinner stroll.

5 DEFENDING CASTLES

'An acceptable level of violence' was a phrase used by a prominent British minister about the part of the United Kingdom for which he was then (in the 1970s) responsible. Contemporary reaction to his remark differed from medieval attitudes in two ways. On the one hand, for all the theorists' distinctions between just and unjust wars, most men in the Middle Ages frankly accepted the existence of violence and war. The modern liberal wish to rule it out of court would have been regarded as hopelessly naive. On the other, it would have been unacceptable to be seen to stand by and let your men suffer violence without retaliation. A lord who could not protect his men was failing in the first duty of lordship. Medieval people would have had more sympathy with a second, and more famous, 20th-century quote: 'Power grows from the barrel of a gun'; violence was a fact of life and only a fool would make no plans to cope with it.

Recently there has been a debate about the defensive role of castles, and their role in war. Until the late 1960s or early 1970s, the orthodox view, as expressed in most general books on castles, was to treat them primarily as fortifications. Medieval history was also focused on the royal documents, and the studies of castles were dominated by the study of royal sites. It was easy to see castles as part of a Whig view of medieval history, where the barons were seen as bad and the kings good. Castles were either military strongholds of violent barons who needed to be curbed by the power of kings and royal officials or royal castles needed as part of this programme. As historians, expanded into economic and social history concentrated more on the wider mechanisms of power, and the barons were seen as having a far more complex role in society. At the same time individual studies pointed to examples of individual castles whose defensive capacity is fairly dubious, and not just from the later Middle Ages. The great towers of the 12th century showed surprising examples of military weakness. Hedingham, for example, had a simple door at the entry and the battlements were difficult to access. The great tower of Trim, started before 1200 in an Ireland always assumed to be a hostile country for its lords, is a most impressive sight. Its side towers, however, make no provision for flanking fire, their walls are thin, and the entrance is almost undefended; it is difficult to see how it could withstand 24 hours of determined assault. Sandal castle was clearly a showpiece of the

13th century, but the curtain walls, which enclose the great hall and major public areas, have no towers and a low-key gatehouse; the defensive display of barbican and towers is reserved for the lord's tower on the old motte, leaving the rest of the castle militarily neglected. A recent study of the magnificent castle of Conway, one of the keys to Edward I's campaigns in Wales, has pointed out that symmetry rather than military effectiveness dictated the design of the arrow loops of the mural towers. Bodiam in particular was dismissed as a military structure because it might not have been capable of withstanding a full siege. The view emerged that the military features of castles were purely symbolic, to be equated with the pomp of town walls too long to be defended or the fashion of decorating a parish church with ornamental battlements.

All this is true but it still does not quite prove the point. Firstly both sides in the debate tend to refer to 'the role of castles' in general when each castle is very much an individual balance of factors. More importantly, there is a tendency to demand that castles should be put in one of only two boxes: militarily effective or not effective; this is either disingenuous or naive. There is no room allowed for grey areas, or the possibility that there might be a sliding scale here. Bodiam is a good case in point. Just because it might prove difficult to defend it against a full-scale siege by a large army, this is no reason to deny its having any military function. It was built in a time of French raids against the south coast of England. Large armies did not carry these out, nor were the men in them either equipped or interested in conducting proper sieges; they would seize a castle if they could take it in a day or night attack, but no more. For this, Bodiam was admirably equipped, and this is stated in the contemporary justification for its existence. Likewise, just because many castles never did figure in war does not mean that they might not have, and so needed to prepare (the doctrine of deterrence) or that they might not have been pressed into service in an emergency.

The view that castles were purely symbolic also misunderstands how complex fortification may be. The multi-storey hotels in Sarajevo or Beirut, the deck-access Rossville Flats in Derry (or Londonderry) were not designed to be fortresses or have any military features, yet they were able to act as such very effectively. This is because of two factors. Firstly, they were acting in a conflict with limited weaponry, essentially small arms, not with either

70 *(above)* Raglan castle, with its flag flying above the castle and over the surrounding land.

artillery or air power. This is of course precisely what prevailed in many of the wars of the Middle Ages. Secondly, they were fortified and held successfully because of the morale of the defenders and the limited nature of the attack, especially in the case of the Rossville Flats. Abstract statements about the ability of a structure to perform in a military way are not as easy to substantiate as they seem.

This leaves two interlocking questions: even if it was not the dominant role for the castle might it not be one of a number of roles and so worth studying? And even if the military aspect was primarily a symbolic statement, why was it chosen as such? (see **2**). Display is a major motive in the design of castles, but that is not necessarily to be distinguished from a military role. It must be significant that the language of display was consistently also the language of military design. Display in itself can also have a military function, to inspire fear in the attacker before he tests the defences. The magnificence of Edward I's castles in north Wales, where each design is different, but all are overwhelmingly powerful, was an end in itself; to demonstrate the power of the English king in Wales and thus to deter Welsh rebellion. Castles were built to serve and reinforce the power of their lords, and power must always have a base in force. The medieval aristocracy worked hard to make their lordship effective and leadership in war remained one of their key functions in society. As such, they were in a position to gauge the military threat that their castles were likely to be called upon to meet. When we look at a castle we can try to reconstruct the defensive role its builder intended, just as we can look for its social or political role. Building a castle involved a series of choices about the way to express its working life, civil and military, as well as balancing these to the resources of the builder. That is why no standard castle could ever exist, why each is a different monument in itself.

WHY DEFEND A CASTLE?

Castles were built to maintain lordship, in times of war as well as peace. War in the Middle Ages, as now, had two main aims. The first was to destroy the enemy's resources, to weaken him and so make him concede things to regain peace and save himself from further loss. The second was to seize land, more or less permanently. In the place of modern aerial bombardment and other means of destruction, medieval armies hit at their enemies' resources by direct pillaging and looting. This was technologically primitive, time-consuming and labour-intensive, but it had the advantage of paying for the army at the same time as impoverishing the enemy; to many in the army it may also have been enjoyable.

Castles were built to prevent, as far as was possible, these two aims. To pillage effectively, an army must disperse into smaller groups and scatter through the countryside. The more it does this, the more vulnerable to counterattack it is from forces which have remained intact in castles; they had slept better and were more sober than the looters. A castle is vital in preventing an invading force from moving to the second objective, the permanent seizure of land, because as long as the lord's flag is still flying over a castle, he cannot be said to have lost his land completely (**70**). The sight will remind the locals that he intends to return, to reward those who have stood by him, and punish those who deserted his cause.

In both cases the castle was a focus for those loyal to its lord, and offered them protection in the short term. If he was to launch a counterattack against the invading army, the castle stood as a centre for his efforts, and as a base for his campaign. In 1173 William the Lion of Scotland invaded the north of England, hoping not only to pillage it but also to seize the Earldom of Northumbria. Jordan of Fantosme records him as debating what to do at one point, and having two choices: 'As long as Prudhoe castle stands we shall never have peace'; and 'Of all the lands you claim, Carlisle is the chief' (**71**). The lesson is clear: the seizure of land without its castles will prove a purely temporary victory. The converse however was also true. In 1199 Richard I agreed to a truce with the French, which left them in possession of the castles that they had captured in recent fighting in Normandy, but gave him the lands around them. In the event Richard had the advantage, for he cut off the garrisons'

71 *(below)* Carlisle castle, target of the Scots in 1173.

72 *(right)* The strategy of the castles built along the Norman frontier in the Vexin; Château Gaillard controls the narrow way between the Seine and the forest of Lyons after Richard lost control of Gisors and the line of the Epte.

attempts to get supplies, or even water, let alone the rents and dues of the land.

The key to castle defence was time. No castle was expected to be impregnable, or to hold out against a determined attack forever; the garrison held out to give their lord time to rally his forces and come to their help. It was perfectly honourable to make an agreement to surrender a besieged castle if it was not relieved within a stated time. A siege was not lightly to be undertaken; dysentery lay in wait for besieging armies in their unsanitary camps. Sieges involved great effort. In 1224 the young King Henry III captured the castle of Bedford, held against him by one of his father's mercenaries. For the siege he drew most of his supplies from the surrounding area, Bedfordshire and Northamptonshire, but he had to send to London, Hertfordshire, Huntingdon, Lincoln, Dorset, Southampton and Gloucestershire for other equipment and weapons.

As a campaign developed, the invading force had a choice. It could retain its mobility by ignoring the castle, but abandon hope of permanent conquest and risk harassment by the garrison. Or it could pursue the siege but then present a clear target for the counter-attack (**72**). In these circumstances, it was logical that the practice arose that a garrison might, with no loss of honour, make a truce with the besiegers; if no help came to them in a stated period (conveyed by them also to their lord), they would surrender. Again it follows that for a lord to abandon a loyal garrison without attempting to relieve them was shameful, just as to abandon the countryside to the enemy was.

I greet you well, letting you know that your brother and his fellowship stand in great jeopardy at Caister, and lack victual... and they fail gunpowder and arrows, and the place sore broken with guns of the other part; so that they, unless they have hasty help, they be like to lose both their lives and the place, to the greatest rebuke to you that ever came to any gentleman ... Do your devoir now and let me send you no more messengers for these matters.

When Caister castle was being attacked by the Duke of Norfolk's men, this was how Margaret Paston wrote to her son John in 1469. The castle and manor lands had been left by Sir John Fastolf to Margaret's husband; the Duke had lost a lawsuit to challenge the will and resorted to other means.

Garrisons were never large, even if reinforced for a full-scale siege. In 1215–16 Hubert de Burgh held Dover castle against a combined army of rebel barons and their French allies for a year with a force, it is said, of 140 knights and many men-at-arms. In the same war, Odiham castle held out for the king with three knights and ten men-at-arms for over a week. Owain Glyndwr's rebellion in 1400 cut the English garrison of Harlech off from help. They held out against a low level of attack for four years, until 1404 when the depleted garrison was split by desertion; by the time the survivors came to surrender, there were only 20 men in all left. As with Dover in 1216, the garrison of Château Gaillard, probably numbering a few hundred in all, held up the whole army of Philip Augustus in his conquest of Normandy for six months after the fall of their outworks. The value of the investment in fortifications is clear, for they multiplied the effective power of the men inside them many times; forces of this size would have been powerless in the field.

DEFENCE BY STRONG POINT

There was a constant battle between the techniques of besieging castles and the design of their defences. By 1100 the simple tactics of rushing or starving out a castle had become elaborated. We hear

73 *(above)* The great tower of Scarborough castle.

74 *(below)* The great tower of Rochester castle from the south-east where the round corner tower marks the rebuilding needed after King John's miners had brought the angle down in the siege of 1216.

of towers taller than the castle walls being rolled up to the defences so that archers could fire into the castle and then men could run on to the walls from plank bridges. There were machines for throwing large stones, the mangonels, powered by the torsion of twisted ropes, which propelled a missile from the end of a long beam of wood like a sling. The response of the castle builders was to reinforce the strength of their walls. Earth banks might be proof against attack, but the timber palisades were easily smashed or burned. Stone was essential, used in walls made as thick as possible. Defence was concentrated in a single tower of massive strength, the great tower (**73**), known later as the keep. The principle was the same as the motte, a strong point of refuge, but the great towers were of stone and usually square, and they dominated castles through the 12th century, from the Tower, *par excellence*, of London, built by William the Conqueror, to the great tower of Dover built by Henry II in the 1180s.

The towers relied on size. They were too high for the movable timber towers of the besiegers to reach up to the battlements, and the walls were too thick for the mangonels to break holes in them. Rochester of the 1120s is 34m (111ft) high to the battlements, with walls 3–3.7m (10–12ft) thick; the tower at Dover is almost 30m (90ft) high, with walls that vary from 5–6.5m (16–21ft) thick. They have only one entrance, raised up to the first- or second-floor level. It needed, therefore, to be reached by a flight of stairs, which was protected behind battlements in a 'forework'; at the top was often a pit spanned by a wooden floor, which could be destroyed if need be. The door, or doors, was held shut by one or more long bars of wood, which ran in and out of long slots in the thickness of the wall on one side; the holes are often still visible today.

The weakness of these towers arose from their very strength. The later 12th century saw a great increase in the use of mercenary foot soldiers in royal armies, and they became expert at sieges. A major development was the technique of mining under walls, propping them up with wooden shoring, so that, when the shoring was set on fire, the walls came crashing down. A new stone-throwing machine, the trebuchet, came into use at the end of the 12th century, which relied, not on torsion, but on a counter-weight to propel the beam and the missile. Ropes were always liable to stretch, so that it was difficult to predict the aim of a mangonel, but

75 *(above)* Beaumaris castle from the air; a concentric design dominated by the great towers along the inner and outer walls.

the same weight of stone would strike the same spot each time with a trebuchet.

The massive thickness of their walls made it difficult to contrive loops for archers in the towers at the same time as crossbow men were becoming more numerous. Besieging archers were able to direct a continuous fire on the tower battlements, the only place from which the defenders could strike back at their attackers. Above all, the great tower put all the defensive eggs in one basket, so that it was the immediate target of all the force of the besiegers. This could even be a political problem. With no discreet exit, it was difficult to leave a tower once a siege had begun; a baron found inside by his king could hardly blame the affair on hot-headed subordinates.

In 1215 King John besieged Rochester castle, capturing the great tower after eight weeks. He did this by mining, bringing down the south-east angle, which was rebuilt afterwards; the corner tower was built half-round rather than square and it still stands as a memorial to the 40 pigs whose fat kindled the fire in the mine beneath (**74**). This is sometimes said to mark the obsolescence of the square great tower, in the face of improved siege craft, particularly mining, although equally there are those who rage against the story of Rochester and its fat pigs for distorting the true

76 *(above)* A longbow man.

importance of towers in general. It is true that there are few great towers in 13th-century castles and that many of them are round, but this single explanation of military need is too simple. To begin with, a number of the round towers, such as Pembroke, which is probably the earliest one in the British Isles, are built on rock, which would have protected them from mining anyway. We must not forget that this is the time when lords began to want their accommodation separated from their halls, and a single tower was now insufficient to provide all they wanted. Be that as it may, the two generations on either side of 1200 saw a shift away from the single strong point as the basis for defence towards making the perimeter the principal fortification, emphasizing the curtain wall.

DEFENCE BY ARCHERY

Curtain wall defence was based on two tactical principles. The first was the use of archery to harass the enemy and break up any concentrations of his troops, especially if they launched a direct assault on the wall. The second was to make it as difficult as possible to get close to the walls, either for people or machines. A subsidiary tactic was that, rather than the enemy breaching the wall and entering the courtyard being the end of the siege, the garrison should be able to fire down into the ward, and indeed make it a death trap. We may start with the provision for archery, which itself involved both the individual positions for the archers, the loops, and the general deployment of them.

The design of the loop depended on the weapon to be used from it. There were two main types of bow available, the crossbow and the longbow, similar in range (effective up to about 100m (328ft), but with an extreme range of twice that), but otherwise each with different properties. The longbow was faster to fire but it required more strength and training even to pull it, and with its high trajectory it needs great skill to aim (**76**). The crossbow has a flatter trajectory and can be sighted along the stock like a gun (**77**). The string is pulled back mechanically and held until released by a trigger, so that it can be used for snap shooting. His slower rate of fire makes a crossbow man vulnerable in the open, but not when behind a wall, while the fact that it can be used with less instruction allows all sorts of people in a garrison to be effective in a siege.

77 *(above)* **A crossbow man.**

The different bows need different loops to fire from. A longbow should be about the height of the archer, and half of this height will be above his eye level when he fires; traversing with a longbow is difficult because it means moving the whole body. The crossbow man can swing his arms round to traverse, but the weight of the bow, if he has to hold it for any time, is difficult to support unaided; a crossbow works well from a kneeling position. The main problem in designing a loop is to produce an opening in the wall which an archer can fire down, and which combines as wide a view of the exterior as possible, while keeping the actual firing slit as narrow as possible so that enemy archers cannot fire in. Experiment has shown that archers can fire one arrow in three through a slit only 5cm (2in) wide, from a range of 25m (82ft), and hit a man standing behind. The field of vision was achieved by widening the slit out behind, to create an embrasure. The larger this embrasure the easier it was for the archer to fire his arrow close to the slit, and so reduce the chances of it hitting the sides on its way. A longbow needs a high embrasure if the archer is to stand within it, a crossbow a wide one, preferably with some support for his weapon at waist height. A second possibility is that the archer stood behind the whole embrasure, to one side so that any incoming arrows missed him, and stepped out to fire when he saw a target. If the garrison was big enough, two men could use each embrasure. For this the embrasure should be set lower, for a longbow in particular.

Deploying archery depends on two principles. The first is that the fields of fire of the individual arrow loops should overlap, and the second is that it is easier to hit someone in a line of men if you fire along the line; it is easier to control the direction of an arrow than its range. This means that it is more effective to shoot at men lined up to attack a wall from the flank than from straight in front. The way to achieve both aims was to deploy archers in towers projecting from the wall, so that they would both look along the wall and would be able to fire from a number of loops in an arc in front of them. Avranches tower in Dover castle was built around 1190 (**78**). It is sited at a vulnerable salient angle of the curtain, which it guards with three tiers of loops, including the battlements. Each tier has sets of triple slits, one firing at 90 degrees to the wall and two at 45 degrees on either side. The height of the embrasures and the stone bracket just below them show they

78 *(right)* Avranches tower, Dover castle. An archery strong point placed to cover an exposed angle of the perimeter.

79 *(below)* The lines of fire from the different levels of the walls and towers of Framlingham castle, guarding the line of approach.

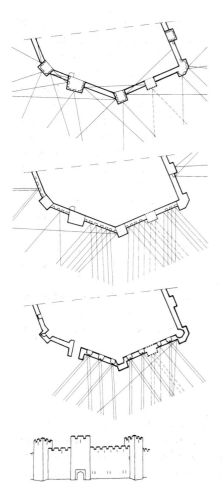

were designed for crossbow men. This idea of a powerful archery tower sited to make a weak spot strong is found in other Angevin royal castles around 1200. Similarly, at the contemporary Framlingham castle, an extra ground-level tier of loops guards the gate approach, by their height designed for longbow men; the loops on the battlements were for crossbows (**79** and see **64**). As the 13th century went on the idea of covering weak areas selectively faded out; castles were more symmetrical in plan, and the curtains tended to have towers at regular intervals. The Avranches type of radiating slits recur in the north-east curtain of Caernarvon in the 1290s, when a most elaborate set of loops was built. These loops appear to give a whole series of firing positions with the minimum number; they require, however, the archers to fire down slits only 5–10cm (2–4in) wide but at least 3m (10ft) long.

DEFENCE OF THE PERIMETER

In some castles a line of square holes through the wall just below the battlements is still visible. These holes are different from the smaller scaffolding holes, and are for heavy beams. Some were probably for beams projecting on the inside of the wall, to widen the wall-walk. Others projected out beyond the wall face and supported a timber front; between the beams were holes through which men could drop rocks on anyone at the foot of the wall below. They are not as common in England as in France, not least, perhaps, because the solid timber front, which protected the dropper of rocks from enemy arrows, stopped archers firing back: the timber was also vulnerable to stones thrown by machines.

80 *(right)* Siting a castle to make it difficult to approach; Beeston castle perched on its rock precipice.

81 *(below)* The great twin-towered gatehouse of Chepstow castle, now known to have been built in the 1190s.

Shooting men outside the walls, or dropping rocks on them if they came close, was no doubt a very satisfying thing to do, but in terms of the broader aims of defence it was better if the besiegers neither came up to the walls, nor were able to bring their machines and mines close at all. The best way of preventing them doing so was by planning the site: putting the castle either on a rock or by surrounding it with water. In 1223 Hubert de Burgh founded a new castle at Montgomery; he rejected the site of the 11th-century castle of Hen Domen on a slight eminence in the valley and put it on a rock hill where it would be harder to approach and safe from mining. In the same decade Ranulf, Earl of Chester erected two new castles, at Beeston (**80**) and Bolingbroke. The first was sited on a rock crag, the second moved down from a hill to the valley bottom, so that its ditches could be filled with water. The most elaborate case of water defences in the early 13th century was designed at Kenilworth (see **44**), where a great dam produced a lake to the south and west of the castle over half a mile long. The fashion was not always carried out successfully in practice. At Greencastle in Co. Down, Hugh de Lacy's mason tried to combine the two ideas: he built a dam for a wet ditch alas for him, he did it in porous rock.

THE DEVELOPMENT OF THE GATEHOUSE

The weakest point in a perimeter is the entrance. It was a surprisingly long time before a consensus emerged as to the solution to this problem. Tree ring research has shown that the great twin-towered outer gatehouse at Chepstow castle must date to very close to 1190 (**81**). The north gate at Dover castle, also with two round towers flanking a gate passage was constructed about the same time, certainly before the great siege of 1216 (**82**). These two examples, and that of Pevensey of essentially the same time, follow two principles of design. One is the use of projecting towers close to the gate to concentrate archery fire on the approaches to it. The second is that the gate should be the front element in a gate passage which could be further defended by other gates, portcullises or bridges. By 1200 these principles, which would be the basis for the major designs from the later 13th century onwards, were therefore in existence and effective; certainly the great gate at Dover performed as well as it might be expected to in the siege. What is remarkable is that these examples were followed, among major castles, by other, different designs: the gates at Château Gaillard had simple openings with no towers projecting beside them to give flank protection, or Dunamase in Ireland, like Chepstow built for William Marshal, has a gate (of the 1190s) to the (present) inner ward set in a single tower. The archery loops at Framlingham castle around 1200 may

82 *(below)* The outer gatehouse of Dover castle, under attack during the siege of 1215–6.

83 *(right)* The basic defences of the 13th-century gatehouse; the twin towers and gate passage, with gates, portcullises and murder hole, at Carrickfergus castle.

have guarded the approach to the gate, but the gate itself is set in a single tower, like a 12th-century example such as Sherborne of the 1120s. The gatehouse at Dover castle was badly damaged in the siege of 1215–16, and was rebuilt in a less vulnerable position elsewhere, as a single tower, oval in plan, in front of the passage. Trim castle has an elaborate example of the same idea, derived from a French model. In four castles of the 1220s that we can see the ideal picked up again in England at Kenilworth, Montgomery, Beeston and Bolingbroke. All have the gate leading to a passage between two projecting rounded towers, the three elements, towers and passage, being bound together into a single building, the gatehouse. This is as clear an example that there were two forces at action in the design of castle defences. One was that in some castles a systematic application of defensive principles was applied, while simultaneously in other castles it could be ignored.

The key to the defence of the gatehouse was the gate passage with a number of different elements (**83** and see **37**). Some of these were of wood, but have left traces in the stonework, so that we can reconstruct the original arrangement even in ruined castles. In fact ruins are often easier to study, for there is no part of the castle more likely to be rebuilt than the gate if the castle continues in use, either to bring its defences up to date, or else to remove the defences in the interests of easier access. The position of the gate itself is shown by the rebate of stone against which it shut, and the holes in the wall at the side for the bars to secure it. A portcullis slid up and down in channels in the walls on either side of the passage; to be lifted fully it needed a slot in the vault or floor over the passage, and, of course, a windlass to lift it. There were often other holes over the passage, which myth-makers imagine were to pour boiling oil or molten lead down on the besiegers' heads. Leaving aside the price of oil or lead, most of the gatehouses, and especially their battlements, were so far from any fire, that the oil, or whatever, would have been pleasantly warm by the time it was dropped. The holes were either

84 *(above)* White Castle gatehouse and towers with archery loops demonstrated to have been designed for flanking fire from long bows.

85 *(below)* A turning bridge.

Pivot

Moat   Pit

for dropping stones, or sometimes for water, not boiling but to put out fires, which the besiegers might light in front of the gate; some might be for counter weights for the portcullis. These elements might all be used, and more than once; the King's Gate at Caernarvon had six portcullises and five gates in succession down the passage. By the last quarter of the 13th century, gatehouses, far from being the weak point of the perimeter, were the most formidable points to attack (**84**).

As the general application of the idea of the twin-towered gate house was not universally seized upon, it is not surprising that it is remarkably difficult to be precise about the development of one element in the gatehouse, the bridge over the ditch in front. We can see the traces of two types of movable bridge in the surviving gates. The true lifting bridge, pivoting at the base of the front wall and lifted with chains, may leave the pivot, but must have holes in the front wall for the chains to pass through. These are not common in original 13th-century castles, partly because of rebuilding perhaps, although they are found, for example, at Beaumaris at the end of the century. The commonest type was probably the turning bridge (**85**). This had a pit within the passage as well as the ditch outside and a wooden bridge, which spanned both, balancing on the outer wall foundation. When a catch was released the weighted inner half fell down into the inner pit, and the outer half lifted against the outer face of the gate, often into a recess contrived for it. This leaves the inner pit, and sometimes the pivot hole in the front wall. The first securely identified and dated surviving example seems to be the Black Gate, Newcastle upon Tyne of 1247–50. Many castles show no signs of the chain holes, pivots or inner pits of movable bridges, and may either have had fixed bridges, or ones that could be dragged back into the passage like ships' gangways.

86 *(below)* The concentric defences of Caerphilly castle, with the inner towers and curtain wall rising above the outer line of defence, so that both can be used together.

Outside the gatehouse proper, one further elaboration might be found: the barbican (see **43** and **82**). This was a wall and ditch in front to provide a first line of defence before the main entrance. If the site lent itself to the plan, the opportunity was sometimes taken to put a turn into the route in, to hold up a sudden rush. In a similar vein, gatehouses to inner and outer courtyards were sometimes staggered in plan, to prevent anyone rushing straight through both.

CONCENTRIC DEFENCE

Until the middle of the 13th century, castles with more than one enclosure tended to present them in succession to the attacker, forcing him to fight through a series of walls. The disadvantage for the defender of this scheme was that the full force of the siege had to be borne by each line of defence in turn. With the construction of Caerphilly from about 1270 we see a conscious attempt to resolve this and have all lines of defence in action together (**86** and see **8**). The outer walls and towers are low enough and the inner curtain close enough to the outer line (reducing the space between almost to a passage) for men on the high inner curtain and towers to fire over the heads of those on the outer curtain. Both curtains are only entered through massive gatehouses, while the whole is set on an island in an artificial lake.

Several of Edward I's castles in north Wales in the succeeding decades follow the same pattern, and together these castles have often been seen as the culmination of castle design as a whole. As a group they are unparalleled, especially when they are combined with those built by lords other than the king, such as Denbigh or Holt. Edward's castles are all different in plan and site, some on rocks and some on the plain. Not only do some have concentric plans and some not, but also there is a conscious attempt to ring the changes in design. They were built to a grand strategic scheme, and this is carried out in their architecture, which is quite self-consciously impressive, from the massive defences to such details as the banded masonry of Caernarvon, recalling the walls of Constantinople itself. The defences are based on powerful towers along the curtains and great, double-towered gatehouses in particular (**88**), although there is nothing there that was not already present at Caerphilly.

LATER DEFENCES

The case for the pre-eminence of the castles of the end of the 13th century is based on their defensive design, but the succeeding centuries were not without development. One invention was that of machicolation at the wall head, particularly of towers. In a sense this was the old idea of wooden hourds, but carried out in stone, with stone arches replacing the projecting beams. It meant, however, carrying the whole battlements, loops and all, forward beyond the line of the wall, and creating a whole fighting gallery, sometimes roofed at that level. It was most used in France (and was much popularized there by Viollet le Duc's 19th-century restorations) but at Warwick castle there is a fine English example. Here the east front was rebuilt at the end of the 14th century, with a fine gatehouse and barbican in the centre and a tower at each end, both capped with machicolated galleries.

The idea is most commonly used on a much smaller scale, however, in the tower houses of northern England, Scotland and Wales (**87**). We have already seen these as the response of a proliferation of small lordships, whose lords had no need to provide accommodation for large households. They did, however, need defence against raids from neighbours and so they built their towers with a defensive capacity that would withstand, not sieges by large armies, but the low level of warfare of their regions. The defence was concentrated on a fireproof vault for the ground floor, a strong door and a fighting gallery at roof level. This was often equipped with machicolations, especially over the door and corbelled out angle turrets, ultimately of French inspiration.

87 *(above)* **The tower house at Belsay. In the 17th century a hall was added to it, on the left.**

GUNS AND CASTLES

The most famous invention (or adoption from the East) in 14th-century warfare was gunpowder. Its early impact on fortification can be seen in three stages. The first is typified by a loop with a circular hole, often with a sighting slit above it, the whole resembling an inverted keyhole. The diameter of the hole is at most 15cm (6in), which would allow a gun of perhaps 10cm (4in) in diameter, firing a ball at most 5cm (2in) across. These were for handguns, to be used not against besiegers' artillery, but as substitutes for bows, against people. They appear in castles of the later 14th century, such as Bodiam, as well as in town walls like Southampton or Canterbury. In France, from the middle of the 15th century, in castles such as Bonaguil or Guerande, we can see the next stage, with the development of wide, horizontal gun ports, meant for guns of heavier calibre. These are mounted at ground level, unlike the lighter pieces, to concentrate a heavier fire on opposing siege works and equipment.

88 *(above)* Harlech castle; the south front dominated by the gatehouse.

The Herberts, when they built Raglan castle, had no reason to feel secure in its possession; there were plenty of others as ruthless as themselves who might try to take it from them. The castle has defensive elements (**89**): the great gatehouse has a fine machicolated fighting gallery, and both it and the great tower have gun loops, while the position of the tower flanking the entrance way is like the sort of contemporary artillery towers apparently built by the English in the last stages of the Hundred Years War in France. The guns are light, however, but above all, the defensive considerations are not allowed to interfere with the overall plan of the castle, nor with such features as the large windows of the state apartments, in full view of an enemy outside the gate. The castle was designed with specific threats in mind. The Herberts might face rioting

89 *(right)* Raglan castle; the gate tower and the great tower; the small holes in the gate tower beside the bridge are early gun loops.

90 *(above)* Deal castle from the air; one of Henry VIII's new artillery forts, excellent for guns but too low and cramped for castle accommodation.

tenants, or a raid from a rival lord's retainers (like the Pastons at Caister), but their power, like that of the king in this period of the Wars of the Roses, would be decided on the battlefield, not by full-scale sieges.

During the early 16th century, ideas developed in Italy about the most effective way to deploy cannon spread to the north of Europe, via France. In the British Isles, partly because of their political links with France and partly because of their own political instability in the 16th century, it was the Scots who first adapted these ideas to castles. The main principle was to arrange the guns in rows, rather than as single pieces, and to deploy them in angular bastions designed to fire along the curtain walls. In the 1530s Sir James Hamilton fortified his new castle of Craignethan for cannon, with a strong curtain wall to the west, thick enough to withstand cannon fire, behind a ditch in the bottom of which he built a caponier, a covered gallery from which guns could control the base. At Stirling in the 1560s, Mary of Guise installed an angled bastion, the 'French Spur' to provide a flanking battery in front of the main defences of this royal castle.

Neither the mounting of heavier guns nor building features specifically for the use of artillery are to be seen in English castles of the 15th century or later.

The 1540s saw a number of artillery works in England, notably the massively expensive series of coastal forts put up by Henry VIII to counter invasion (**90**). At Carlisle, the Half Moon battery was built to reinforce the inner defences. In the 1560s the great artillery defences of Berwick were built against the Scots. None of these were in castles that were the residences of lords or kings, however. They were either in forts manned entirely by paid garrisons, or, like Carlisle, in strategic royal castles occupied by royal officers. Castles and artillery were architecturally and socially incompatible.

Raglan was typical of the 15th century in the low priority it gave to defence. This can also be seen in the way some defensive features were used. Lord Cromwell's great tower at Tattershall has an array of machicolations at the top of the main walls; the Bishop of Winchester's tower at Farnham, built a little later in the 1470s, has a line of them over the gate. In both cases the machicolations are not carried round the angle towers, where they would have been of most military use, but visually they take the form of a decorative line of corbelling.

THE END OF CASTLE BUILDING

One of the oldest beliefs about castles is that the adoption of artillery brought about the end of castle building. In terms of defences and the role of castles in grand 16th-century wars, this is true. Stirling and Craignethan exposed one of the crucial problems of combining artillery (as opposed to hand gun) defences with castles. The new weapon demanded new fortifications: low walls, wide ditches, flanking bastions and batteries of guns (91). These needed a large perimeter to deploy and a large garrison of specialist gunners to work them. The design of residences could not be combined with dignity into the low, wide perimeters of gun defences; the latter had to be pushed out beyond the front of the castle. Nor could the gunners be socially incorporated into the lord's household in the way that the men who defended a medieval castle could. Guns and gunners were both expensive and conspicuous. The expense meant that as the 16th century wore on, and artillery became more sophisticated, only kings of major states could afford to have them. The increasingly dictatorial kings of the time, typified in England by the Tudor dynasty in general and Henry VIII in particular, were liable to become instantly suspicious of any aristocrat who added artillery defences to his castle. If artillery was for the defence of the state, it should be in royal hands, otherwise it was likely to be used against him. Building artillery defences on to your old castle was a sure way to the scaffold.

A second cause for the end of castles has been proposed: the new fashions in architecture of the Renaissance in Europe north of the Alps. The grim castle gave way to a building ornamented with many windows, and the symmetrical front was imposed on the informality of the castle, or so runs the idea. In fact the symmetrical show front is present from the mid-14th century at the latest. We can see an early example at Maxstoke, built by William de Clinton, Earl of Huntingdon, by about 1345. The east front has a wet moat and a magnificent, high gatehouse. The needs of the second- and third-floor chambers in the gatehouse, however, required double light windows, in spite of the military weakening that this meant. The curtain wall on either side of the gate is low, perhaps deliberately so, to emphasize the gatehouse and the lord's private tower across the courtyard. Nor do the walls rise from the moat but from a berm or platform which would have given an attacker who had crossed the moat a convenient resting place; the doors in the two side rooms built against the gatehouse open on to this berm, and show that it was original. Maxstoke is but an early example of the show front with central gatehouse and corner towers, which were very popular for centuries. The grand hall front of Kenilworth was carefully balanced with a tower at either end of the hall, each with octagonal buttresses (see **62**). The tower between the hall and the lodgings is a fake, a screen for the change of angle between the two ranges and not a true, self-contained structure as a tower should be. It was needed to create the façade and its symmetry. The hall and chambers at Bodiam are identifiable because of their windows, as is the hall at Bolton. The chambers of Thornbury, itself built in the early 16th century with a show front designed around the gate and angle towers, are a riot of invention and a display of glass. The medieval design of a front, with angle towers and a central gate house formed one of the basic types for 16th-century houses, whether of the French Renaissance as at Chambord, or of English courtiers' houses, as at Titchfield in the 1540s or Burleigh towards the end of the century. The internal elements of the grand castle continued to be present in great houses right through the 16th century. Burleigh House has a great hall and suites of rooms for the lord and guests. It can be read in the same way, for ceremony and accommodation as a medieval castle. Blenheim 'castle', a grand Baroque creation built around 1700 can also, but it is about the last in this manner. The problem for the castle was neither military function nor architectural style but the style of life it was designed to serve. The castle was a place of ceremonial social power, maintained by large and expensive households containing many

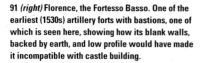

91 *(right)* Florence, the Fortesso Basso. One of the earliest (1530s) artillery forts with bastions, one of which is seen here, showing how its blank walls, backed by earth, and low profile would have made it incompatible with castle building.

grades of servants. During the 17th century this was increasingly out of fashion for various reasons: cost, a differing attitude to service, a changing role for the aristocracy in politics and a fashion for more direct social relations among others.

17th-century Ireland sheds an interesting light on the issues. From the middle of the 16th to the end of the 17th century, Ireland was the scene of widespread and vicious war, ultimately between the forces of a Protestant English state and a Catholic Irish aristocracy. Only with the advent of Cromwell and his artillery train in the late 1640s did big guns play a role in this war, but before then castles had changed. Great aristocrats, English and Irish, had started to build houses in the new manner when they could afford them. In areas where a new gentry was uneasily intruded into the country, notably with the Plantation of Ulster in the early 17th century, the newcomers often chose to erect tower houses, small castles, to protect themselves. They proved useless for this in the rebellion of 1641, but the failure was nothing to do with their defensive features, or lack of them; it was because the defenders were simply either too few or isolated and afraid. Nonetheless, castles played a role in the Civil wars of the 1640s. Castle building, and the occupation of many of them, came to an end during the century, particularly after the two triumphs of the English forces after 1660 and 1690. This was not for military or fashionable reasons, but because of social shifts. In Scotland the possession of a tower was evidence of an honourable ancestry and possession of the land (see **102**). In Ireland, the new English aristocracy who seized the great majority of land as a result of their success did so at the end of a bitter struggle. They wanted to emphasize that their regime was new, opposed to all the the old order stood for, and was here to stay. They slighted the old towers, took the building materials away and built new houses in their place. It was the Georgian house, not artillery, which rang the death knell for the castle in Ireland.

6 VISITING, DESCRIBING AND STUDYING CASTLES

The castles we visit now are either ruins, or else much altered by later use. The world of the men who built them is gone, and therefore to visit a castle with any sort of enquiry in mind requires an act of the imagination to reconstruct its history and original appearance or use. The detail of the individual castle is a first step, understanding in a general way how castles worked is another. A consideration of the evidence, whether written down by contemporaries (the history), or that of the site and remains themselves (the archaeology), of the castle forms the beginning. However, the details must be understood against the background of the normal, general pattern of life in castles as a whole, and this is best learned, not from chronicles or administrative documents, or the archaeology, but from contemporary works of literature.

CASTLES IN MEDIEVAL LITERATURE

One of the roots of recent work on castles has been to try to approach them through what contemporaries wrote about them. This has focused not on the political or institutional legal record, the charters and royal documentation of government, but more on contemporary descriptions. One of the conclusions has been to argue that the emphasis on the private nature of the castle's role in politics has been overplayed in the past and that, for example, the fortified town and the castle were seen as different facets of the same thing. In part this is a re-play of the old baronial/royal military/symbolic argument: in part it draws too strong a line between the private and the public. This is again reverting to the political role, because a castle was never a 'private' place except in terms of its role in administration. A castle was always accessible to people outside the immediate household, whether to a grand social event in a great castle, or the manor court or even the village church in a lesser one. One of the interesting results of this has been to see the symbols that the castle seems to have often represented. To some churchmen, undoubtedly castles represented a rival power to that of the church and the result is a hostile press for them, which fuelled much of the 'bad baron' myth. On the other hand the castle and the enclosed place were powerful images. They occur in the Bible and the same word 'castellum' was used for them as for the contemporary castle; some of the aura must have transferred to the

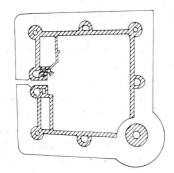

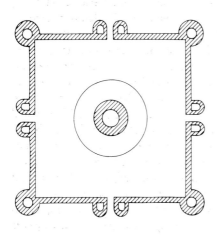

92 *(above)* Dourdan castle and the castle of Lady Jealousy in the *Romance of the Rose* compared.

castle as a result. There is also a powerful image of the enclosed space, town or castle as place of refuge and order, of safety from violence and chaos outside. As such we find it as an allegory for the chastity of the church, or of women against the assault of men.

Some of the best medieval descriptions of castles are to be found in the works of fiction. Not only are the *chansons de geste* and romances filled with incidental references to castles, for as aristocratic stories, castles are the proper setting for events, but also occasionally they give a full set-piece description of a castle. Sometimes this is deliberately to heighten the effect of the magical, as in the *Romance of Sir Orfeo*, a reworking of the Orpheus myth. The hero penetrates to the Underworld, to the King of the Dead's castle. This is no ordinary castle, but one built of crystal, gold and precious stones. The formality of the allegory in the *Romance of the Rose* is continued in the careful symmetry of the castle built by the Lady Jealousy to guard the Roses. It is a perfect square with corner towers, and gates on each of the four walls; it had a high round, great tower in the centre of the courtyard. Written in the middle of the 13th century, it reflected the round towers and symmetry of contemporary castles around Paris, such as Dourdan (**92**).

The finest of all these descriptions occurs in one of the great English poems of the 14th century, 'Sir Gawain and the Green Knight'. It combines a description of individual architectural features and a precise sense of location for events, with the overall impressions a fine castle was meant to convey to a visitor. Of course, it is a work of fiction; the castle is not a real one (although some scholars have tried to argue that it is based on an actual one), but a composite account, meant to convey the impression that this is a splendid castle, magnificent yet not impossible. The castle belongs to Sir Bertilak, magician and beheader, husband of the would-be seductress of Gawain; Gawain is the tempted and tested hero, epitome of chivalry and virtue, who stays with Sir Bertilak over the Christmas holiday on his way to his great test at the New Year. It is 'the comeliest castle that ever a knight owned'.

Gawain arrives at the castle across its park and is confronted by its defences, whose strength the poet stresses: the curtain walls rise high from a double moat, while the entrance is guarded by a barbican, a drawbridge and a machicolated gatehouse, with gates and portcullis, all in a state of defence when he arrives. When he is allowed through the gate, the various actions take place in carefully specified parts of the castle. On arrival his horse is led away to the stable across the courtyard while lower servants conduct him to the hall. Here the knights and upper members of the lord's household greet him, but Sir Bertilak himself is not there. He does Gawain the honour of coming down from his own chamber, and then escorting him to the room that he will occupy during his stay. There he washes and the household provides him with new clothes, and a meal at a table and chair brought in for him to use. It is Christmas Eve, so that the whole company go off to Mass in the castle chapel, where Gawain meets up with Sir Bertilak again, and also sees his wife for the first time, in her private pew. After Mass the inner household retire for entertainment to the lord's great chamber, before going to bed. Thereafter, there is a clear distinction drawn between the private events, which take place in Gawain's chamber, and the public feasts and entertainment in the great hall, which is also where Sir Bertilak and Gawain openly exchange their pledges.

The poet emphasizes the location of the events, partly because it increases the sense of immediacy and normality of the story, in contrast to the hidden magic and fantasy beneath it. It also allows him to indulge his interest in the art of polite behaviour and hospitality, as he does in his descriptions of the details of the hunts. It mattered where the two principals met and struck bargains, just as it mattered that there would be a difference between the outdoor servants and the inner household; the hall, great chamber and private chamber all had their place in social ranks. So too it mattered that the castle was where Sir Bertilak could display his wealth and power in clothes and hangings on the wall; we may note that it was in these rather than in furniture. The poet's imagination may lead him away from what is strictly probable. When Gawain looks at the castle from the edge of the moat, he is described as seeing the great hall within, with its turrets, crenellations and pinnacles. This is in fact unlikely; from his viewpoint, if the curtain walls are as high as the poet says they are, he could only have seen the top of the roof at best; how was he to know that he was looking at the great hall? (**94**). The answer may be that it was the most commanding roof and therefore that of the hall, or else that, by poetic licence, when he saw a castle, he 'saw' the hall that he knew must be there and be the core of the castle he was looking at (**93**).

ſe nouuelle⸗ Albion

93 *(right)* Louis d'Orleans held prisoner in the
Tower of London as shown in a manuscript of
c.1500. As with literary descriptions, the portrayal
of the castle and scale of the figures are
subordinated to the message.

THE HISTORY OF AN INDIVIDUAL CASTLE

The documents that the historian considers are usually the
utilitarian documents written by royal or baronial administrators,
or else the more formal, 'published' chronicles and works of
literature. The first group tend to receive the most academic
attention, because they are the sources that give us the basic
material about an individual castle's development. They include the
surveys of the buildings, undertaken from time to time or the
accounts of the money spent on their building or repair. To use
them we must remember some rules, which are derived from the
reasons the documents were written in the first place. Surveys,
particularly those that lead up to requests for money, may
exaggerate the position; this is a commonplace of any bureaucracy.
Added to this natural tendency is a problem of language; some
people may be confused when a castle is described in Latin as
ruinatum. This does not mean 'ruined' but 'in need of repair'.
Similarly lands attached to it may be called *vastata*, meaning
'producing no income', not 'devastated'. Another trap may be to
assume that, because the king or lord ordered some work to be
done, his wishes were automatically carried out.

At least when an account roll records that money was spent on
work, we may be confident that the work was done. It may not
always be clear what the work precisely was or where it was done;
all too often, the clerks are prepared simply to note that money was

94 *(right)* Beaumaris castle from the edge of the moat; Gawain's view of Sir Bertilak's castle.

95 *(below)* The outer gatehouse of Carlisle. The contract for its construction, made in 1378 with the mason John Lewyn, provides a detailed description of it. In the event, when it was built it was re-designed and enlarged.

spent 'on the works of the castle of …' with no further explanation. That said, there are many very detailed rolls, with a wealth of information about what work was done on which parts of the castle, when and at what cost, or by which workmen (**95**). In royal castles, the annual records may be so complete that we can argue from the absence of references that no significant work was done at a certain time. Similarly, in connection with baronial castles, it may be argued that in the lord's absence, or due to the fact that the lord was a minor that it is unlikely that work went on in a certain period. This is the core of the dating of the history both of individual castles, and then by combining them, of the general development. It is clear, however, that the much greater volume of royal documents that survive, as opposed to baronial ones, has meant an almost inevitable concentration on the study of royal castles.

If we turn to chronicles, this means wars, for chronicles, like the modern newspaper headlines, dearly love a war. They are full of castle sieges, but curiously to the modern mind, have few systematic descriptions of the castles themselves. King Philip Augustus of France spent his whole life fighting to expel Henry II, Richard I and John, as Kings of England, but also Dukes of Normandy and Counts of Anjou, from their French lands. His wars culminated in the siege of Château Gaillard in 1203–4, where he attacked the castle, which was the finest work of Richard who had humiliated him on Crusade; as we saw, his capture of the castle opened up the core of Normandy to his armies (**96**). William the Breton, in his life of Philip, devotes over two thousand words to the siege, and we might expect him to start with a description of the famous castle that presented his hero with such a problem and achievement. His story is filled with incident, the suffering of non-combatants left to starve between the siege-works and the castle defences, or how the middle ward was captured by a young soldier who climbed up to a chapel window on his companion's back, but it is only if you know the layout of the castle that you can follow the narrative. The capture of the chapel was a judgement on John for having built it beside the castle latrines; history is didactic, teaching lessons of virtue in life. Personal motives and actions are more important than dispassionate narrative.

Chronicles in their incidents record many individual details about castles. From the frequent accounts of the efforts put into sieges we can see in general how important castles were thought to be in war. From the sequence of events in campaigns, we can work out their role in the overall strategy of attack and defence. Only rarely does a more personal attitude to a castle creep in, as in Jean de Joinville's *Life of St Louis of France*, when he describes his own departure with the king on Crusade in 1248. On a practical note, he tells how he brought all his men before him in his castle at Joinville, and settled all the claims they had on his estate before he set out. As he prepared for his journey, however, he says he never allowed himself to see Joinville, 'for fear that my heart might be filled with longing at the thought of my lovely castle and the two children I had left behind'. The administrative role is commonplace, but the homesickness is rarely expressed.

THE ARCHAEOLOGY OF A CASTLE

The equivalent work for the archaeologist is the detailed record and analysis of the fabric of the walls, either above or below ground. This will have two aims. The first is to note the presence of individual features, such as doors, windows or fireplaces on the domestic side, or the arrow loops, gates, etc., on the military side, and their relationship to each other. This means initially recording the plans of walls and rooms, and putting them together into large plans floor by floor, and then putting the plans together with the heights, in elevations of walls and sections through the buildings (see **17**). This puts a three-dimensional record of the whole together. The second aim is to note the original structure and then to disentangle from it the evidence of change, the blocked windows or doors, or the ones that cut through an earlier wall, and the way older walls have been destroyed, or new ones added on to the old. If the walls are ashlar, built of stones cut to a rectangular shape and laid in regular rows, or courses, this will be relatively easy (**97, 98**). The coursing will be interrupted, and the new stones often do not match well at the junctions. If the stones are not cut to shape, and not laid in regular courses (rubble), detecting change is much more difficult; archaeologists working on the rubble-built castles of the north and west of Britain, especially Scotland and Ireland, envy those where the good ashlar masonry is common.

These are the nuts and bolts of castle studies expanded by excavation to uncover the foundations of walls or other buried remains, such as basements. Excavation is also the only means of discovering the artefacts and environmental remains that tell us of the economic infrastructure of the castle, or to trace the long-decayed remains of wooden structures. The basic aim must be to work out the stages or periods of construction of a castle, and then to say when each was carried out, as accurately as the evidence permits. Ideally, the physical remains and the documents combine to complement each other. Often, the historian finds references to work that cannot now be traced on the ground, or the archaeologist is faced with an undocumented castle that he must date from any fashionable details of the stonework, or by excavation for datable artefacts associated with them. Inevitably such matters dominate professional work, for if we do not have these basics securely worked out, we cannot be sure of any general statements. It is all too easy, however, to leave it at that, and not to push on to explanations as to why and how the castle was built or used.

VISITING A CASTLE NOWADAYS

The modern traveller may imitate Gawain in his visit to a castle, although with differences: Gawain had to ride across a deserted landscape in midwinter to reach Sir Bertilak's castle, but he was at least welcomed by a courteous porter, and not charged for entry. He saw the castle from some way off, dominating the countryside from a height, before he approached it through the hunting park, and

96 *(above)* Château Gaillard above the river Seine, built in three years, 1196–8.

97 *(below)* Two blocked doors visible in good masonry (at Wells cathedral). The lower one is shown to be original by the way its arch and sides fit with the stones around it; the upper one is an insertion because it has no proper frame and it cuts through the original stones.

reached the road that led to the gate. This is the one area where the poet seriously departs from life: no castle was set in a deserted landscape. Nowadays few castles are far from a road or away from a town or village. Approaching a castle we may bear two questions in mind. The first is the choice of the site. This may have been connected to the natural topography of the area concerned, either features, such as a ford or route way, or else to the pattern of lands held by the owner when he built it. While a castle was often rebuilt or continued in use because it was already there, at the beginning of its life someone chose to put it in that particular place. Some of the reasoning behind that choice may still be understood from its position in the landscape now. The second point to bear in mind is that we have often lost much of the outer shell of a castle. They were the heads of estates, and this meant that there would have been buildings of perishable materials, now vanished, in their immediate vicinity. These might be the farm buildings or they might be the houses of the people who worked there, but castles were rarely set in an empty field. Sir Bertilak's park is all that the poet mentioned, because that was the only feature of the periphery that concerned his intensely aristocratic story. Besides the physical surroundings, castles were meant to dominate the area and people around them, either by the threat of force or by the arts of political or social influence, as well as the powers of a landlord.

THE CASTLE FROM THE OUTSIDE

It is useful to think about the siting of the castle both in the contemporary landscape and, if possible, in the landscape when it was built and in use. Nowadays the park refers to cars rather than deer but it is a start to think of the sort of land around, whether good arable or grazing. Roads and routes may have changed little since the medieval period, and the relationship of the castle to them is important. One of the common ideas under this heading is that

98 *(right)* A wall (to the right) constructed against an earlier one (at Barnard castle).

if a castle is placed by a bridge or ford, this was to 'command' it. It is often very difficult to understand this when we examine the site in detail. Is there supposed to have been a police post manned from the castle? Are the garrison supposed to have shot from the castle anyone crossing the bridge without permission? Remember the range of a medieval bow; anyone more than 200m (655ft) from the castle was not running a great risk. What about night time? As always the control is of peaceful people; travellers and merchants who were prepared for the sake of peace to pay a toll. It is far more likely that this is a matter of domination and display by the lords than real control.

Like Gawain, the first tangible contact a visitor has with a castle is with the outer line of its defences. It was here that the poet initially was able to show that Sir Bertilak lived in a first-rate one by listing the individual features that such a castle of the period might

99 *(above)* Dover castle from the east. The two lines of defensive curtain walls studded with towers (lowered c.1800) surround the great tower which dominates the whole.

be expected to have. We can begin to assess any castle in the same way. The obvious starting point is the line of approach, which is normally clearly dictated by the lie of the land of the site (**99**). The approach that leads to the castle gate may not be the simplest, as in the case of Dover where Hubert de Burgh deliberately rebuilt the gatehouse attacked in the great siege of 1215–16 in a less accessible position to protect it, a clear example of the balance between ease of access and defence.

The lord, as the Middle Ages wore on, was presented with increasingly elaborate defensive systems, from water-filled moats to massive gatehouses. The site might dictate his choice (water-filled ditches are difficult on rocky hill tops) but most were as much a matter of cost as anything. The amount he put into defence and the care with which features such as the arrow loops were sited to cover vulnerable points, all give indications as to the extent to which the military side of the castle was central to his thinking. The same can be seen in individual features: the examples of the great tower have been mentioned earlier, which were built to serve as residences rather than as points of last resort in a siege, as shown by the details of their defensive organization. Two exercises in military imagination would have been involved: to speculate as to how an army might attack the castle and then to look for the methods by which such an attack was meant to be countered. This also involves a consideration of the sort of equipment that might be deployed against the defenders, as well as their ability to maintain supplies through a long siege, crucially of water.

THE LIVING ACCOMMODATION

The castle defences form the shell of the inner core, but few people should confine their visit to them. On his arrival, Gawain was escorted to the great hall of the castle, while his horse was led to the stables. This is the key to understanding the layout of the interior of a castle. The great hall both linked the upper household with the lower and it was also the social centre of the whole (**100**). Its size and the elaboration will identify it still, just as it did for Gawain from outside the castle: it will have the largest windows possible, and inside often a large fireplace and a double latrine to cope with the needs of the crowds who would have used it. Its entrance from the courtyard is both likely to be elaborate and at one end of the structure; in the later Middle Ages this will correspond to the physical orientation of the social side of the hall.

The upper end will communicate with the upper household's accommodation, while the lower end will lead to the service rooms, notably the kitchen. The higher-class rooms will be marked by the quality of their windows and other carved details, and by the presence of fireplaces and private latrines. The service rooms will lack these comforts, while the great kitchen fireplace can hardly be confused with one to heat a single chamber. These are the sort of things which we can note when we attempt to reconstruct in our mind the way the castle was meant to work. As with the defensive aspects, of course, the time dimension is vital; what was a luxurious layout in the 12th century would have been primitive to the point of shame in the 14th, just as a powerful fortress of the 12th century would have fallen quickly to the siege techniques of the later period. Lying behind it however, is the size of the lord's household and the elaboration of the provision he wanted to make for it.

The essential point in assessing a castle is to appreciate at every turn that the builder was making choices. Behind every castle is a mind and a purpose which it was uniquely designed to serve. If we compare castles with the other great buildings of the Middle Ages,

100 *(above)* Ludlow castle; the hall lies centrally at the end of the inner court between the service and chamber blocks.

the abbeys and cathedrals, the point may be clarified. The purpose of all churches was the same, the worship of the Christian God. The means might be different, from a small parish church to a cathedral, from a rich Benedictine monastery to the poverty and mission of a Friary, but their essential purpose is the same. Castles were built to serve a whole variety of purposes, to have a military, political, social and economic role. The emphasis on each of these aspects varied according to the wishes of the lord who built it. He was presented with different options, in military or domestic design, which he had to balance against his resources if he wished to be prudent. The site, the military strength and the domestic accommodation all tell us of the sort of life that the lord expected to live in the castle. The subsequent alterations (and few castles were not subject to almost continuous change) tell us how the later generations either maintained the original role or changed it.

This is what makes castles so interesting, that they are both so variable and yet are built according to certain clear principles. They provide us with an immediate point of contact with the Middle Ages, either with the mind of individuals or with the possibility of reconstructing the daily routine of life for a considerable section of the population. It is a world distant from ours but not so far as all that. Members of a modern secular society find the life of a monk difficult to envisage; the medieval peasant existing on the bread line of subsistence agriculture is equally remote. The means of exercising power have changed from the Middle Ages to now, but the fact of power has not. Much of the modern European world was created in the period: languages, states, ranks; the form and technology of a book go back to this time, as does the idea of a university, such as the one in which this book is written. The men

101 *(above)* Sandal castle; the motte, stair and inner barbican at the foot of the motte, exposed as part of a most ambitious programme of excavation.

102 *(below)* Amisfield, Dumfries; the old tower and the new house. The old tower has been restored to preserve it.

who dominated that world did so from their castles with aims, if not methods, which we can readily understand.

THE FUTURE FOR CASTLES

We, the Mayor, Sheriffs, Burgesses and Commonality of the County of the Town of Carrickfergus, beg leave to state to your Excellency, that the Castle of Carrickfergus is a building of great antiquity, a memorable and interesting monument of ancient times. That it is the only ancient fort on this part of the island which now remains in a state of preservation, and in the troubles of former ages afforded protection and security to our ancestors. That we have heard with concern of an intention of converting it into a barrack, and that workmen are actually employed to break out a number of windows in the walls which will not only deface its ancient and respectable appearance, but also, we apprehend, endanger the entire building. That from the great thickness of the walls and the smallness of the rooms, we consider it particularly unfit and inconvenient for the purpose of the barrack, and that we are well informed the addition of £200 to the sum now to be expended on it would erect more suitable and better accommodations for the military on the site of the former barracks or any other situation which might be deemed eligible. That the Corporation of Carrickfergus has always been forward to testify their loyalty to his Majesty, and good disposition to the military when quartered among them by every means in their power ... May it therefore please your Excellency to take the above into consideration, and to give such orders and directions relative there to as may prevent the defacing and demolishing of an ancient fort dear to the inhabitants of this Corporation from the records and remembrances of former times, and an interesting object of attention to the antiquary and even to the strangers.

This plea was written to the Lord Lieutenant of Ireland more than two hundred years ago, on 22 January 1793, and its arguments for conservation are very familiar. They are all there: local pride, academic interest, tourist potential, and even the appeal that a small amount of extra expenditure elsewhere would give a much better result. Like so many since, they failed to persuade the government (**102**). The future of castles lies in three areas: conservation of sites, their study and the presentation of the knowledge to the public.

The conservation of castles is a surprisingly contentious topic; not so much through conflict between those who wish to remove them and conservationists, but about the actual policy of conservation. Ruined stone walls do not last well by themselves, but need to be made stable and waterproof if they are to last. Earthworks are prone to erosion by the feet of visitors or cattle, while the growth of trees on them may obscure them while they are alive and tear them up if they fall. The old standards of preservation of the remains 'as they were found' with no restoration were expensive and required considerable skill and thought. As such, in an era of cost-cutting, examples of bad practice have crept back. Apart from simple mistakes, there are real points of disagreement. The first source of tension is between restoration and conservation. In some cases, it is argued that the 'as found' approach has left us with shapeless and uninterpretable ruins, and there are examples to prove the point. The result is a pressure to restore. Neither extreme is good. We need to be clear whether what we are looking at, and studying is work of the period, not a modern piece of work. Conservation of ruins covered in vegetation also hides evidence of the original; conserving what we do not understand is not easily defended either.

For the castles outside the state net, the pressures are different. It may be that they have survived crude attempts at conservation or restoration in return for benign neglect. Deliberate destruction as a possibility, usually for public projects such as new roads, is probably a receding threat. It has been replaced by that of full-scale restoration, especially that of tower houses for conversion to dwelling houses (**101**). Covering the walls with plaster, inevitable in the interior at least, and often applied to the outside for weather proofing, obviously hides all the evidence of the original stonework. New floors and the installation of services inevitably destroy evidence above and below ground. Against this is the likelihood that the castle will moulder into collapse. A total photographic record, along with excavation, may be a compromise solution.

The study of castles has changed greatly over the last thirty years. The earliest of these shifts was the debate over the military

103 *(above)* Carrickfergus castle from the north east. The artillery battery and musket loops along the wall tops are part of the work carried out in spite of the local protests in 1793.

importance of castles, which has cropped up from time to time in this book. By breaking up the theory that castles were built for military use and that their history revolved around political events, this led to recognition of the variety of purposes they served and the complexity of interpreting them. The result was to examine castles, either individually or as a group, in terms of the various roles which they played in contemporary life. Different scholars attached differing weights to each of these roles and studied castles from differing viewpoints. The result was to open up the subject greatly.

This has been followed by a collapse in state funding for traditional research projects on individual castles. The biggest symptom of this retreat has been the end of the policy of grand excavation of castles, which has been abandoned in the name of conservation. It seems unlikely, on the grounds of cost, that we will see many of such large-scale excavations, as those at Sandal castle, which examined the whole of the inner courtyard of the castle. Excavation will undoubtedly continue to be used to look for the earliest phases of a castle's history and, of course, to trace the perishable wooden buildings of castles built of timber and earth, but it will only be small-scale. In conjunction with the various methods of geophysical survey, it is to be hoped that we shall see the excavation of the outer areas of castles, the store buildings and the outer courts that supported the inner area.

Research has been forced to focus on other approaches. It could be argued that academic views of castles have changed to reflect wider debates outside the topic. The view of castles as essentially related to the function of the King (or state) belongs to the post-war era when state management was unchallenged; this was also the high point of state conservation and management of the castles themselves. One of these is the environmental position of the castle, and the role of it and its lord in land management. This coincides with a broadening of our view of power and its maintenance. The stress on the environment, on symbolism as opposed to military power and the emphasis on the locality contrasted with the royal power are all such new issues. Castles are about power and the deconstructing of systems of power is a very typical issue for debate at the end of the 20th century.

It was only the chance that Carrickfergus castle was still was used by the state in 1793 that caused the Mayor to write to the Lord Lieutenant, because by then most of the royal castles had been abandoned or sold off. It is different now for castles are mostly Ancient Monuments and the state is very much concerned with their fate. The arguments may not have changed since 1793 but the context has. State involvement has been enormously beneficial to castles and their study, bringing preservation, money and research to them, but it has not come without strings. The castles taken into state care and open to the public are usually the large and well-preserved ones. Earthwork castles and the lesser stone ones are the ones left out of the net. This is inevitable and not be criticized but it does reinforce the generic image of the castle as a large stone structure in the public mind. Unfortunately the sense of the ordinariness of the castle, represented by the lesser ones, is lost.

A second consequence of the state involvement is that castles are now expected to earn money, where in the Middle Ages they were places which cost money. Both for financial reasons and because it is public money which maintains them, they are expected to attract the greatest number of visitors possible. No longer is it acceptable to complain that 'the result of the low admission charge is to admit a rough class of visitor who tend to keep the more intelligent class away', in the words of the custodian at Dover castle in 1930. This has meant a shift in the presentation to the visitor of information about castles. The 1960s saw the pinnacle of a policy which saw the aiming of information at visitors who were as academic as the writers of it. This was represented by guidebooks with complex plans (impossible to manage in wind or rain) and written in an unrelenting prose. They had to go, to be replaced something more 'popular'. In a spectacular case of snobbery, this was deemed to be not just less academic in approach but also in content; they talked down to the public. A great and very commendable effort has been made to involve castles with school teaching, not only directly, to teach about the Middle Ages, but also to bring in other topics such as the mathematics of measurement. Unfortunately it has been largely aimed at Primary level at the expense of later years. This aligns with the general decline of medieval studies in later years at school, and universities, in the face of a history or literature syllabus focused almost exclusively on modern times.

Two pictures still dominate the general image of the medieval castle. The first is that of war, of knights and sieges, while the second is of brutality, exemplified by the change of the word 'donjon', or great tower, into the modern 'dungeon'. Both have their place, but it must be admitted that their survival, as hardy as the image of the horns on Viking helmets and other historical myths, is a condemnation of academics for failing to convey their changed views to the public. This goes hand in hand with the wider contempt for the Middle Ages as a whole. Medieval is a term of abuse, instead of what it should be, a word recalling the period when modern Europe was forged and which gave us our languages, basic laws and political institutions along with many technological inventions from mills to clocks. Many castles were never besieged, or if they were, only once or twice in as many centuries. Most lords were only held prisoners for ransom and would then be usually reasonably treated, being rich; the poor they normally hanged. A better image is of the busy workplace, not a factory but a centre of power and political domination of the land and people around it. The castle in its heyday was a crowded place, a continuous assault on all the visitor's five senses at once, and a meeting place of the richest men of the land and all their inferiors. Its defences remind us that a competitive and aggressive military aristocracy dominated Europe of the Middle Ages. The elaborate accommodation provided for the lord's household, and the number of the people involved in the life of the castle reflects the way that the royal or aristocratic power in medieval Europe differed from that of other civilizations. It was not based on a single state and a supreme ruler, like the great Empires, but on a mixture of competition and bargains between the lords and their inferiors. Leadership in Europe always involved a strong element of consent and required rulers to earn the respect of the ruled if they were to succeed. Castles were one of their main instruments in this.

PLACES TO VISIT

The British Isles contain hundreds of castle sites, and it would be hopeless to offer more than a selection here. I have chosen this list on the basis of there being substantial stone remains surviving above ground, with a bias towards castles in the hands of public bodies and therefore open to the visiting public, and also a dash of personal prejudice. The asterisk marks those sites that are not necessarily freely open to the public.

ENGLAND

Acton Burnell (Shropshire) Late 13th-century manor house in the form of a large single tower subdivided into hall and chambers on two floors.

Ashby-de-la-Zouche (Leicestershire) Sprawling, ill-defended site with domestic remains of the later Middle Ages, culminating in a large residential tower of the later 15th century.

Barnard Castle (Durham) Fine site over the river Tees, occupied by inner ward with 13th-century domestic range, rebuilt (with the defences) in the fourteenth century. Outer wards and gatehouse divide it from the town.

Beeston (Cheshire) A cliff-top site overlooking the Cheshire plain. Two circuits of walls, the inner marked by a fine gatehouse of the 1220s.

Belsay (Northumberland) Late 14th-century tower house with an early 17th-century house added.

Bodiam (East Sussex) Classic late 14th-century quadrangular castle, well preserved and set in an extensive artificial lake.

Bolingbroke (Lincolnshire) A new site of the 1220s, set in the low ground below the hill of the earlier castle. A nearly regular six-sided courtyard with towers at the angles and a two-towered gatehouse.

Bolton (North Yorkshire) A new castle of the late 14th century. A rectangle, with square corner tower, houses a complex series of lodgings.

Bridgnorth (Shropshire) A small Henry II great tower, leaning alarmingly after an attempt to blow it up in the Civil War.

Brough (Cumbria) 12th-century great tower heightened in the later 13th, with lodgings surrounding the courtyard from the 13th to 17th centuries.

Carlisle (Cumbria) A castle with remains of every period from the 12th-century great tower to modern times (it remained in use as a barrack until the later 20th century), notably the late 14th-century gatehouse.

Castle Acre (Norfolk) A late 11th-century enclosure for a semi-fortified manor house strengthened in the 12th century with a stone wall and a great tower.

Christchurch (Dorset) Motte and stone tower, and the well-preserved remains of a late 12th-century stone hall and chamber block.

Colchester (Essex) Massive great tower built by William I, now housing a museum.

Conisbrough (South Yorkshire) A stone wall, affected by later subsidence, encloses foundations of a great hall and a fine private great tower.

Corfe (Dorset) Set on a steep hill, with remains from the late 11th-century enclosure and hall, early 12th-century great tower, very early 13th-century 'Gloriette' royal lodgings, and later thirteenth-century curtain walls and gatehouses.

Dover (Kent) Remains of every period from the 12th-century great tower (the largest in England) to the curtain walls of the late 12th and 13th centuries, including the Constable gate, to modern times.

Dunstanburgh (Northumberland) Remote, cliff-top site with a vast enclosing wall of the early 14th century; the gatehouse rebuilt later in the century.

Edlingham (Northumberland) Manorial hall of c.1300 with a residential tower added in the 14th century, and the courtyard built up.

Exeter (Devon) Late 11th-century enclosure in an angle of the Roman town wall; the gate tower shows the use of Anglo-Saxon (as opposed to Norman) building techniques.

Framlingham (Suffolk) The present remains almost entirely date to after the destruction of the castle in the late 12th century, an enclosure wall which was one of the first to dispense with a great tower.

Goodrich (Hereford & Worcester) Set high above the Wye valley, apart from a 12th-century tower, the remains are all those of a massively defended castle of c.1300 with the domestic accommodation well preserved.

Hadleigh (Essex) Earlier enclosure strongly re-fortified by Edward III in the later 14th century to defend the coast.

Hedingham* (Essex) Finely-built 12th-century great tower.

Hylton (Tyne & Wear) 14th-century combination of the tower house plan and accommodation with a show front.

Kenilworth (Warwick) The 12th-century castle (marked now by the great tower), had extensive water defences added in the 13th, and then the great hall, services and lodgings rebuilt in the late 14th century.

Kirby Muxloe (Leicestershire) Late 15th-century castle, never finished, built of brick within a rectangular moat.

Launceston (Cornwall) Stone wall surrounding the top of a high motte.

Lewes (East Sussex) One of only two castles in England with two mottes, one of which has a stone wall around the top; the 12th-century gatehouse had a barbican added in the 14th century.

Lincoln The castle is open to the public, including the towers. Built by William the Conqueror. The Bishop's palace is a good example of hall and chamber planning of the 13th century and later.

Tower of London Every period from the late 11th-century great tower to the completion of the double line of curtain walls in the late 13th century.

Longthorpe (Cambridgeshire) Small 13th-century tower notable for its wall paintings.

Ludlow (Shropshire) Enclosure of c.1100 with a single gate tower. Great hall and two blocks of lodgings of the late 13th century.

Lydford (Devon) A small earthen enclosure succeeded by a stone tower and courtyard, used not for residence (therefore not a true castle?) but as a court and prison.

Maxstoke (West Midlands) Strong manor house of the 14th century, with a rectangular courtyard, corner towers and gatehouse, enclosing a great hall and lodgings, set within a moat.

Middleham (North Yorkshire) 12th-century great tower surrounded by a 13th–14th-century curtain wall and lodgings.

Minster Lovell (Oxfordshire) 15th-century manor house.

Newcastle upon Tyne (Tyne & Wear) The castle is now divided by (among other things) a railway, but the 12th-century great tower and the 13th-century gatehouse survive.

Norham (Northumberland) 12th-century great tower and curtain walls rebuilt in the 16th century for defence by cannon.

Norwich (Norfolk) Very large 12th-century great tower, now much rebuilt.

Nunney (Somerset) Rectangular tower with projecting round towers at the angles surrounded by a moat; a 14th-century building after the French fashion.

Okehampton (Devon) 12th-century tower on a partly artificial motte, forming the core to a castle with great hall and lodgings rebuilt in the 14th century.

Old Sarum (Wiltshire) Massive earthwork set within an Iron Age hillfort, and containing a courtyard house of the 12th century.

Orford (Suffolk) Polygonal great tower built by Henry II in 1165–73, set within a walled enclosure, now marked by earthworks.

Peak (Derbyshire) Small 12th-century tower in an enclosure on a hill top.

Pevensey (East Sussex) 13th-century enclosure around the 12th-century tower, set within a late Roman fort.

Portchester (Hampshire) The inner ward of the castle is in the angle of a late Roman fort, marked by a 12th-century great tower and lodgings, mainly of the late 14th century.

Restormel (Cornwall) The 12th-century (?) inner ring wall was filled with the accommodation for the Earl of Cornwall in the later 13th century.

Richmond (North Yorkshire) Large late 11th-century stone enclosure on a cliff over the river Swale, containing the contemporary hall and chamber. A great tower was added in the 12th century and further domestic accommodation to the chamber in the 14th.

Rochester (Kent) The first castle was an enclosure in the angle of the Roman town wall, later reinforced by the great tower started in 1127.

Sandal (South Yorkshire) The original motte was converted in the 13th century into a magnificent show tower for the lord, while the bailey contained the hall and other public buildings.

Scarborough (North Yorkshire) A cliff-top enclosure guarded by the 12th-century great tower and the later gate and barbican.

Sherborne (Dorset) The 12th-century enclosure (with gate tower) contains the early 12th-century courtyard house of Bishop Roger of Salisbury.

Stokesay* (Shropshire) A classic minor castle or manor house of the 13th century. The moat encloses a hall and chamber block with a chamber tower added at the end of the century.

Tamworth (Staffordshire) An early motte and bailey castle. The motte top is now occupied by a 17th-century house within a 12th-century enclosure wall; the bailey is guarded by a 13th-century gatehouse and later stone bridge.

Tattershall (Lincolnshire) The 15th-century great, brick-built chamber tower dominates the castle moats.

Wardour (Wiltshire) A late 14th-century castle built around a hexagonal courtyard, with a show front for the hall.

Warkworth (Northumberland) The early 13th-century curtain wall encloses buildings of all periods, especially the great late 14th-century lord's chamber tower, on the site of a motte.

Warwick A magnificent show front of the late 14th century with machicolated gatehouse and corner towers in the French style. The interior much altered during the continuous post-medieval occupation.

York The motte is matched by another across the river Ouse, and crowned by a 13th-century quatrefoil stone tower.

SCOTLAND

Bothwell (Strathclyde) The castle is dominated by the great 13th-century round tower which was a part of an ambitious scheme which was uncompleted. The present buildings of the enclosure date from the 14th and 15th centuries.

Caerlaverock (Dumfries & Galloway) Laid out in the plan of a triangle in c.1277, much of the present curtain wall and towers are of the 15th century with 17th-century buildings within.

Claypotts (Tayside) A complex tower house of the later 16th century, equipped for defence with guns.

Craignethan (Strathclyde) A strong tower house of the early 16th century provided with outer defences for cannon.

Dirleton (Lothian) A mid-13th-century enclosure dominated by a round great chamber tower; the present great hall is of the 15th century.

Doune (Central) A 14th-century castle, with a great hall and service block dominated by the gatehouse which contains the lord's lodging.

Dundonald (Strathclyde) The 13th-century twin-towered gate house was converted into a tower house in the 14th century.

Dunstaffnage (Strathclyde) A 13th-century enclosure, with slightly projecting towers, set on a confined rock in the Highlands.

Hermitage (Borders) A strong tower house, contrived by infilling a 14th-century courtyard, and adapted for defence by guns.

Inverlochy (Highland) 13th-century rectangular enclosure defended by round corner towers.

Kildrummy (Grampian) A towered curtain wall, with a gatehouse added, possibly by Edward I c.1300 during the War of Independence.

Kirkwall (Orkney) The Earl's Palace combines fine Renaissance decoration with castle planning around 1600.

Morton (Dumfries & Galloway) 14th-century castle built around the first-floor hall, with a gate tower attached.

Rothesay (Strathclyde) An early 13th-century, simple, circular enclosure with towers added later in the same century.

Stirling (Central) A very fine display of royal castle planning with the latest 16th-century Renaissance decoration.

Tantallon (Lothian) The cliff-top site is protected by a massive 14th-century curtain wall, with the hall and chamber tower behind.

Threave (Dumfries & Galloway) Large, late 14th-century tower house, surrounded by an artillery defence of c.1450, which cut off the hall from the tower. Built on an island.

As well as these castles, there are many tower houses of the late 14th to 16th centuries preserved throughout most of Scotland. It would be impossible to list them all here and very difficult to select individuals for inclusion.

WALES

Beaumaris (Anglesey) The last of the great Edward I castles in Wales, begun 1295 and never finished. It is perfectly symmetrical and concentric with two large gatehouses, and a protected dock for supply by sea.

Caernarvon (Gwynedd) Begun in 1283, to be the head of Edward I's principality, but never fully completed. An irregular oval in plan, with polygonal towers and banded masonry probably built to imitate the walls of Constantinople.

Caerphilly (Mid-Glamorgan) Begun just before 1270, and continued on for a generation after, it is one of the first castles planned with concentric defences from the first, as well as a broad artificial lake, now restored.

Carew (Dyfed) Built around 1300, the strong curtain wall has massive towers; the great hall dates from the 15th century, while the whole was converted into a country house in the 16th century.

Carreg Cennen (Dyfed) Originally a Welsh stronghold, it was fortified in the late 13th and 14th centuries by the English with concentric curtain walls and a large gatehouse.

Castell y Bere (Gwynedd) Most of the remains are those of a 13th-century Welsh castle, with two D-shaped residential towers on a rock crag, but later refortified by Edward I.

Chepstow (Gwent) The core of the castle is a hall tower of the late 11th century, to which were added successive defences in the late 12th and earlier 13th centuries. At the end of the 13th century it saw a massive new hall and chamber block added, with a lord's private tower.

Cilgerran (Dyfed) The strong curtain wall and massive towers date from the earlier 13th century.

Conway (Gwynedd) Built in five seasons, 1283–7, it commands the crossing of the Conway river. It has two courtyards along the crest of the rock on which it is built, with eight massive towers, but because of the narrow site, no true gatehouse, uniquely for a castle of Edward I in Wales.

Criccieth (Gwynedd) The castle was started by the Welsh king Llywelyn, who may have built the present inner curtain wall, possibly including the gatehouse. Its fortifications were strengthened by later Welsh lords and then by Edward I.

Denbigh (Clwyd) Perhaps a little neglected because, although it formed part of the series of castles built under Edward I, it was not royal but baronial. The castle is dominated by the remarkable triple-towered and decorated gatehouse.

Dolbadarn (Gwynedd) A castle of the Welsh king Llywelyn the Great, probably built in the earlier 13th century. The main feature is the large round tower.

Dolforwyn (Powys) Built by Llywelyn in 1273–7, to challenge the English castle of Montgomery. On the hill top are two strong towers, one round and one square, linked by a curtain wall.

Dolwyddelan (Gwynedd) A square tower built by the Welsh.

Ewloe (Clwyd) Another Welsh castle with the typical D-shaped residential tower.

Flint (Clwyd) One of the first of Edward I's castles in Wales, started in 1277. The inner courtyard is square with a round, residential tower at one corner.

Grosmont (Gwent) A hall block of the years after 1200 had a curtain wall with strong towers and gatehouse added c.1220.

Harlech (Gwynedd) One of Edward I's castles, built 1283–9. A cliff-top site defended by concentric curtain walls and a massive gatehouse.

Kidwelly (Dyfed) A 12th-century enclosure had large towers added in the later 13th century, and then an outer line of defence, with a large gatehouse shortly after 1300.

Montgomery (Powys) Built as a front line castle of the Border in 1223–31, it has two courtyards along the hill top, the inner one with an early example of a twin-towered gatehouse.

Oystermouth (West Glamorgan) A castle of the 13th century, with very well preserved curtain walls, although the gatehouse has lost its towers.

Pembroke (Dyfed) The bulk of the castle dates from around 1200, with a large vaulted round tower for the lord, as well as an early gatehouse.

Raglan (Gwent) One of the few well preserved castles completely of the 15th century. It has a polygonal tower for the lord, two courtyards, separated by the great hall, and a massive gatehouse.

Rhuddlan (Clwyd) One of the first of the series of castles built by Edward I, it incorporated a dock leading to the canalized river Clwyd in the outer of its two concentric defences. The inner wall has two twin-towered gatehouses set at diagonally opposed corners.

St David's Palace (Dyfed) A fine late 13th-century example of a lightly fortified but well decorated house with halls and chapel set around a courtyard.

Skenfrith (Gwent) An early 13th-century castle, set in a valley to exploit water defences, it also has a fine round tower for the lord's residence.

Tretower (Powys) The early 13th-century castle with a strong round tower was succeeded by a manor house in the 14th century.

White Castle (Gwent) The small enclosure was strongly fortified with towers and archery slits in the early 13th century.

IRELAND

Adare (Limerick) Late 12th-century hall in an enclosure with a simple gate. An inner enclosure may be early, as may the tower within it, but it has 15th-century features.

Askeaton (Limerick) Island enclosure containing a 15th-century great hall built over an earlier one, and a large hall and chamber block possibly early 16th century.

Athenry (Galway) 13th-century enclosure with angle towers and a fine first-floor hall.

Ballintubber (Roscommon) Large enclosure with polygonal angle towers and a surprisingly small gatehouse.

Ballymoon (Carlow) Rectangular enclosure (possibly unfinished) with evidence for ranges of fine lodgings but little defence.

Ballymote (Sligo) The best example in Ireland of a late 13th-century castle built as a formal rectangle with angle towers and a twin-towered gatehouse.

Cahir (Tipperary) An island castle with a 15th-century hall on earlier foundations, and 15th–16th-century defences.

Carlingford (Louth) An enclosure of c.1200, with a later cross-wall for a great hall and chamber block.

Carrickfergus (Antrim) Inner enclosure with great tower of the late 12th century, followed by two enclosures of the earlier 13th century; continuously occupied until 1926.

Castle Roche (Louth) Cliff-top enclosure of the 1230s with a gatehouse chamber block linked to the great hall.

Clonmacnois (Westmeath) Motte and bailey with a later stone wall and hall house on the motte.

Dunamase (Laois) Hill-top site with two successive enclosures, with a barbican; the top occupied by a great tower.

Dundrum (Down) Inner courtyard of late 12th century with a round great tower. Outer enclosure added in the late Middle Ages.

Dunluce (Antrim) Dramatic site on a rock stack over the sea. Inner curtain and towers, 14th century, occupied by a major manor house of c.1600.

Ferns (Wexford) Great tower with round corner turrets of a type peculiar to Leinster in the earlier 13th century.

Grannagh (Kilkenny) Rectangular enclosure with angle towers providing a facade towards the river, controlled by guns. 15th-century hall and chamber block.

Greencastle (Donegal) Built c.1300 as a small version of an Edward I castle in Wales. Polygonal tower and gatehouse.

Greencastle (Down) Earlier 13th-century enclosure with angle towers and a first-floor hall.

Harry Avery's castle (Tyrone) Late 14th-century castle with a residential tower resembling a gatehouse.

Nenagh (Tipperary) Fine round lord's residential tower started c.1200 and heightened later in the 13th century.

Newcastle West* (Limerick) Parts of the castle scattered through several modern properties: a fine early 14th-century hall, a first-floor one of the 15th-century and a chamber block.

Roscommon Rectangular enclosure of the later 13th century with angle towers and twin-towered gatehouse, rebuilt as a country house in the 16th century.

Trim (Meath) Largest castle in Ireland. Major great tower of c.1200, with curtain walls and gatehouses dating to the early 13th century.

Like Scotland, there are hundreds of tower houses throughout most of the Irish countryside, which it would be impossible to mention here; some are in state care or otherwise open to the public, while many others are equally well preserved.

FURTHER READING

The most important development in the study of castles in the British Isles is the flourishing of the Castles Study Group. It was still young in 1992 but with a larger membership now, combining 'amateurs' and 'professionals'. Its Newsletter is an essential source for all the latest ideas, debates and results on the subject; it can be accessed most easily via www.castlestudiesgroup.org.uk

Castles have attracted writers for at least a hundred years and the literature on them is vast. J R Kenyon has produced three bibliographies of all the material published on the subject, published as Council for British Archaeology Research Reports, numbers 25 (1978), 53 (1983) and 72 (1990).

The shifts of academic interest in castles over the last thirty years can be followed in general books on castles. The traditional view, that they were military and political buildngs, dominated by royal castles and policy, derives from the magisterial work, H M Colvin (general editor): *A History of the King's Works* (6 volumes, HMSO, 1963–82, especially the first two, medieval volumes). The material in volume I on Edward I's castles in Wales is also published separately as A J Taylor: *The Welsh Castles of Edward I* (Hambledon, 1986). This was followed by five general surveys, all chronological in organization, presenting the story of the development of castles through time, and covering England and Wales. The earliest was R A Brown: *English Castles* (Batsford, 1976). He also wrote *Castles from the Air* (Cambridge, 1989), which is both a list of individual photographs and accounts (of uneven quality) and a fine summarizing introduction to the topic. C P S Platt: *The Castle in Medieval England and Wales* (Seeker

& Warburg, 1982) concentrates rather more on the social side of castles, while D J C King: *The Castle in England and Wales* (Croom Helm, 1988) is very much about the military side of castles. A smaller book is B K Davison: *The Observer's Book of Castles* (Warne, 1979). Although they dominated the subject, they were by no means the only sources available in their time. Other books focused either on a period or on the more civil side of castles. D F Renn produced a gazetteer, *Norman Castles in Britain* (John Baker, 1968) which set out to gather information on every castle in the British Isles built before 1216. M Wood wrote *The English Medieval House* (Phoenix) in 1965, which discussed the history of individual features rather than the whole. P A Faulkner wrote two crucial articles on domestic planning in *Archaeological Journal*: from the 12th to the 14th centuries in volume 115 for 1958 (pp.150–83), and the 14th century in volume 120 for 1963. The story of castles as houses is continued in M Howard: *The Early Tudor Country House* (George Philip, 1987) and M Girouard: *The English Country House* (Penguin, 1970).

Historical sources for lordship, especially its social side, are the subject of F M Stenton: *The First Century of English Feudalism* (Oxford, 1961), M W Labarge: *The Baronial Household of the Thirteenth Century* (Harvester, 1980) and C Given Wilson: *English Nobility* (Routledge & Kegan Paul, 1987).

The end of the 1980s saw this mould breaking. N J G Pounds: *The medieval castle in England and Wales* (Cambridge, 1990) stressed the administrative and social networks of early castles, especially baronial ones, based on documentation. J R Kenyon in *Medieval Fortifications* (Leicester University Press, 1990) took as his subject the results of excavations on castles. M W Thompson: *The Decline of the Castle* (Cambridge, 1987) considers the period after 1300; it was followed by *The rise of the castle* (Cambridge, 1991). P Barker and R A Higham: *Timber castles* (Batsford, 1992) is as much about earthwork castles as timber and therefore covers a previously much neglected group. O H Creighton: *Castles in the landscape* (Continuum, 2002) puts castles into their social and physical context, towns, villages, administrative units etc. R Liddiard: *Landscapes of lordship* (B A R, 2000) discusses the castles of Norfolk and how they relate to the natural and managed landscape. C Coulson: *Castles in medieval society* (O U P, 2003) and A Wheatley: *The idea of the castle* (York, 2004) discuss the contemporary documentary sources about castles. M Johnson: *Behind the castle gate* (Routledge, 2002) discusses castles in the light of more general archaeological theory.

These works concentrate very much on England and Wales, looking often more to France than to Scotland or Ireland. For Scotland S Cruden: *The Scottish Castle* (Nelson, 1960) is still a basic source, while more recently C Tabraham has written: *Scottish Castles and Fortifications* (HMSO, Edinburgh, 1986). An alternative view of Welsh castles – those built by the Welsh lords, rather than by English lords in Wales – is provided by D J C King: 'The defence of Wales', in Archaeologia Cambrensis, vol.126, 1977, pp.1–16. A collection of important essays is found in R Avent & J R Kenyon: *Castles in Wales and the Marches* (University of Wales, Cardiff, 1987). Two books have appeared recently on Ireland. T E McNeill: *Castles in Ireland* (Routledge 1997) and P D Sweetman: *The medieval castles of Ireland* (Collins/Boydell & Brewer, 2000). Castle studies in the two countries are linked in the collection of essays, J R Kenyon & K. O'Conor: *The medieval castle in Ireland and Wales* (Dublin, 2003).There are even more studies of individual castles than general works. Most obviously are the guidebooks available at many of the sites in state care – of English Heritage or others. Longer (not to say massive in their detail) recent monographs include M R McCarthy et al: *Carlisle Castle* (Historic Buildings and Monuments Commission for England, 1990) or G Beresford: *Goltho*, from the same publishers in 1987. The last is an excavation report, and other excavations which might be (quite invidiously) picked out would be P Mayes & L A S Butler: *Sandal Castle* (Wakefield, 1983), because of its scale; P A Barker & R A Higham: *Hen Domen, a Timber Castle on the English-Welsh Border* (London, 1982) for its detailed techniques of excavation; or J G Coad et al.: 'Excavations at Castle Acre', in Archaeological Journal, volumes 139 for 1982 (pp. 138–301) and 144 for 1987 (pp. 256–307) for their information on early castles. Peter Ellis has published two major earlier excavations on castles: *Beeston castle, Cheshire* (Historic Buildings and Monuments Commission for England, 1993) and *Ludgershall castle, Wiltshire* (Devizes, 2000). J Darlington (ed.): *Stafford castle: survey, excavation and research 1978-98, volume I* (Stafford, 2001) is a very full survey of the earthwork remains of, and around, a castle.

GLOSSARY

almoner The officer in the lord's household responsible for his charity.

bailey A courtyard in a castle.

barbican An outer fortification in front of the gate of a castle.

buttery One of the two service rooms typically attached to a castle hall, used for dispensing drink.

caponier A covered gallery running across a ditch, housing guns to fire along the ditch.

caput The chief place in a lordship, where the court was held.

chamber A relatively private room (as opposed to the hall), used either for sleeping or for everyday life.

chamberlain An officer in the lord's household, originally responsible for the control of the lord's chamber, and then for financial affairs.

chancellor The officer of the household responsible for writing letters and charters.

constable The official in charge of the castle, especially when the lord is absent.

curtain wall The wall around the perimeter of a castle or one of its courtyards.

demesne The part of the lord's estate which he farmed directly, rather than leasing out.

embrasure The opening in a wall behind a window or an arrow loop.

great chamber The room which served for the formal everyday life of a lord, more private than the hall, but not for sleeping.

great tower The most important tower in the castle and often its strongest point, from the 16th century often called the keep.

hall The room in the castle reserved for the public life of the lord, courts and solemn feasts.

hourd A timber gallery carried on beams projecting from the top of a wall; the defenders could drop stones to the base of the wall through holes in the gallery floor.

hundred Subdivision of the county combining a number of parishes.

keep A 16th-century term for what is referred to in medieval documents as the great tower.

loop The actual slit in a wall for firing an arrow (or bullet) through.

machicolation A line of stones projecting from the top of a wall. An outer wall is carried on these stones, between which are holes through which defenders can drop stones on to the base of the wall below. A permanent, stone version of a hourd.

mangonel A stone-throwing engine powered by twisted ropes.

marshal The official responsible for the lord's horses and soldiers.

merlon The length of parapet between the openings of a battlement.

mews A building or yard where the hawks are kept.

motte A large, normally round, flat-topped, mound of earth which supported a tower or other building and acted as the strongest point in a castle.

palisade A strong wooden fence.

pantry The service room attached to the hall used for the preparation of food.

portcullis A wooden grille (often covered in metal) which could be raised or lowered in grooves on either side of a gate passage to act as a gate, but less easily forced open.

postern gate A small gate, usually only wide enough for people on foot, which acted as a back door to a castle.

seneschal The lord's key officer and deputy.

tiltyard Long, narrow yard devoted to jousting.

tower house Small castle consisting mainly or entirely of a single tower.

trebuchet Stone-throwing engine powered by counterpoise weights.

ward Courtyard in a castle.

INDEX